FINDING MARIA

By Peter Szabo

"**Achingly beautiful**. *Finding Maria* is a heartfelt, honest look at love and loss across generations of a family."
— Melissa Wuske, *Foreword Reviews*

"The timeless ritual of cleaning out the apartment of a deceased grandparent, becomes a moving and multi-layered history of a family, of Hungarian Jewry, of the Holocaust and communism, and of an extraordinary woman. With graceful prose and a sure sense of narrative, Peter Szabo shares his discovery of his family's past, of their suffering and bravery, betrayals and the catastrophic loses. When the apartment is empty, the possessions distributed, and the door on one life is closed, the reader is left with memories that seem almost personal, so clearly do these lives nearly become our own."
— Marianne Szegedy-Maszak, author of *I Kiss Your Hands Many Times: Hearts, Souls, and Wars in Hungary* (Spiegel & Grau)

"This is a marvelous story that reflects upon the powerful rapport between grandson and grandmother and how that connection impacts the quality of life for both. What grandson and grandparent share in this story insures that the social isolation and loneliness that has become synonymous with many as they age is lessened and a rich cultural history is passed on to a new generation captured through the appreciation for an 'elusive chance for friendship.' "
— Mark Meridy, Executive Director of DOROT

"We have reached that time in history that the last of the Holocaust survivors are leaving us and some are taking their stories with them. It is our last chance to hear from their mouths what they experienced.... While neither Szabo or his grandmother are simple characters, he has chosen to tell the story in simple prose. That does not mean, however, that the prose is not beautiful, because it is and it takes you away. I believe that in its simplicity the story comes across as more honest and most intense."
— Amos Lassen, *Reviews by Amos Lassen*

"In *Finding Maria*, Peter Szabo perceptively describes how he discovers the elusive relationship between generations and among family members. It is a story of discovery: Of family history, of the struggles of European Jewry in the Holocaust, of Jewish identity. As readers, we share in the struggle to preserve, maintain, and transmit Jewish identity, despite significant odds. The book carries a universal message, as well: How do we learn from previous generations? How is our life enriched by the experiences of our forebears? With great skill, Szabo teaches us how we can live in the past and in the present at the same time."
— Fred Reiner, Rabbi Emeritus of Temple Sinai, Washington D.C., and author of *Standing at Sinai*

FINDING MARIA

A Young Man's Search for His Grandmother, and Himself

Peter Szabo

Copyright © 2016 by Peter Szabo

All rights reserved. No part of this book may be used or reproduced in any manner whatsoever without written permission except in the case of brief quotations embodied in critical articles or reviews.

Excerpts from *The Politics of Genocide: The Holocaust in Hungary,* by Randolph L. Braham, copyright 1993 by Randolph L. Braham, used by permission.

ISBN 978-0-9913274-4-7

Front cover book design by Daniel Middleton, Scribe Freelance

Photo of Maria from the author's collection

Chickadee Prince Logo by Garrett Gilchrist

Visit us at www.ChickadeePrince.com

First Printing

PETER SZABO

FINDING MARIA

PETER SZABO's writing has appeared in numerous publications, including *Bioscience, Maryland Historical Magazine, Socio-Analysis,* and *Gotham Gazette*. His work spans such varied topics as the civil rights leadership of noted 1960s activist Gloria Richardson Dandridge, open space preservation, the rise of the Working Families Party, behavior dynamics in strategic planning, urban revitalization, and racism. His volume of poetry, *Death and Life*, was published in 2014. He lives in New York City with his wife and children.

FINDING MARIA

A Young Man's Search for His Grandmother, and Himself

Chickadee Prince Books
New York

*For Maria,
and for my family*

FINDING MARIA

[1]

Long after we knew she would never return to it, my father and my aunt gave up my grandmother's apartment. On a clear spring morning, I headed out to Queens to help them empty the place of her things. My aunt Eve loved gossip and confrontation. She held strong, often strange, opinions. My father was steady and gentle; his temper rare, though hot. When they were together, some conflict always emerged, and I worried about what might arise between the two of them over the course of several days in that small space. At Times Square, I boarded an R train, the local. I opened the *Times* and started a story about the discovery of George Mallory's frozen body on Everest, but I found it difficult to concentrate, my attention drifting to Queens and flitting once or twice to the nursing home that now housed my grandmother. As the train passed Jackson Heights, I began concocting excuses for not showing up. "Dad, it was terrible, the train broke down. We were stuck for hours! Maybe tomorrow." But that only took care of one day, I told myself. "Dad, I'm so sorry, I forgot about this project I have to finish by Thursday." But I didn't have a bit of work at the time. "Dad, you'll never guess who came to town out of the blue!" Of course, then he would want to see them for dinner. I slumped in the seat. No, no excuse would do. He needed me there, to help him deal with Eve, to help him with the decisions. Decisions had become especially difficult for him of late. Most days, surrounded by ever-growing piles of paper, he spent hours in his study playing computer solitaire. I meditated on the white pulse of subway tunnel lights, and as I exited at Continental Avenue and walked down 108th Street toward the apartment, I daydreamed of nothing.

I scanned the row of identical garden apartments on her block, trying to remember which was hers. Eve's Hungarian-accented staccato drew me toward one of the buildings, and soon I heard my father's murmurs escaping through an open window. At the doorstep I paused. I looked down the street toward the dead end. Beyond a tangle of vines and weedy trees ran the Grand Central Parkway, and I stood for a time and listened to the rush of cars, a thousand exhales. An old man shuffled by, walking a tiny dog. He glanced at me, expressionless. I surveyed the small front yard, relaxing. Suddenly, I saw my grandmother convulsing in her nursing home bed, the white sheets receding from her, folding, then falling to the floor, her pale blue gown fluttering back down to her pale white skin after each sharp movement. Nurses arrive. Staff rush her to the hospital across the street. Urinary tract infection. Another gruesome incident. Eve spoke of suing the nursing home, but it was just bluster. She was more grandiose than vindictive. "These sorts of things happen in nursing homes," my father said, as if the event had involved a stranger.

When my grandmother's health collapsed a year earlier, I experienced a slashing pain. I managed the pain by seeking distance. Yet, just when I thought I had established mental distance, chronological distance, any sense of separation from the pain I could manufacture, some new crisis confronted me with the measure of what had been lost–her infectious hunger for life, her caring gaze, the touch of her fingers on my elbow as we walked, her stories, her friendship. The nursing home incidents seemed like messages from her, as if she had been trying to maintain contact by the only means she had left. They touched me like abrasives on a wound. Damn orderlies, I thought as I stared at the yard, do your goddamn job and clean her catheter. I took a long, deep breath. If I did not go into the apartment, I would not have to think of her, I reasoned. But after considering one last feeble excuse and a dash to the subway, I turned back to the door, knocked, and entered.

[2]

The visits with my grandmother started with a simple phone call seven years earlier. The receiver clattered on the base as someone answered the phone. Then, nothing.

"Granny?" I said.

"Yes, hello-oh?"

"Granny, it's your grandson, Peter!" I said, shouting into the telephone.

"Oh, Peter!" she said, her tone jumping up and down over the syllables. "Dear Peter darling, let me turn down the television." Game-show applause quieted in the background. "Dear Peter, I cannot tell you how happy I am to hear your voice!"

"Oh, I just wanted to see how you were doing," I said, in my best earnest-grandson imitation.

"Thank you, dear. I am wonderful. Today I was at the Museum of Modern Art and Saturday at the Metropolitan Opera with Irene. And you, how are you?"

"Not bad, work is okay." I could see how easy this was going to be, speaking just in headlines. Really, it was the act of phoning that mattered, I told myself. I had worried the call might become long and involved, but now I sensed that I would be back to my evening in minutes. Then, on an impulse

I could not squelch in time, I said, "Do you think you might want to meet up some weekend?"

I regretted the idea as soon as I set it loose. It had been a long time since I had been in touch with her, and I felt I should make it up to her in some way. But getting together might mean an hour for coffee, or maybe even sacrificing lunch, when all I wanted to do on my weekend trips to New York was to see friends. I held my breath.

"When?" she said.

Damn, I thought, hesitating. "Any time in the next month or so."

"I might have an extra opera ticket on the twenty-first, in the afternoon," she said.

I squelched a groan. The opera meant the whole afternoon.

"That sounds great."

"We could meet for lunch at Josephina," she said. "No, let's meet at the fountain, then lunch. You know the big fountain in the Lincoln Center?"

"Yes," I said, making a weak effort to hide my sense of resignation.

"Let's meet there at eleven o'clock, dear. I will have a ticket for you." Her excitement consoled me some, and I started to ask about her summer plans. "Wonderful, dear Peter," she said before I could speak. "I am so happy you called. See you on the twenty-first. Bye, dear." Then the line went silent.

Her name was Maria, but we called her Granny, a moniker that conjured up an image of a simple old lady in an Appalachian hollow. She was about as different from that as could be imagined, and the dissonance between name and person generated emotional distance. She had left Hungary at midlife and spoke and behaved like a foreigner. Her visits to our house in a comfortable Maryland suburb brought her difference into relief. She came by bus, which arrived like a spaceship amidst the car world in which I lived. We would wait at the station, a small square building surrounded by large tan buses with red script letters spilling across their length, T-r-a-i-l-w-a-y-s, the bottom of the Y sweeping back underneath the name. I used to stare at the people getting off the bus. Rumpled, dark, tough-looking, they were not like my neighbors and friends. Then she would appear and the driver would extend his hand and help her down the last step. Her impossibly large suitcase would emerge from the belly of the bus, and soon we would be on our way to the house.

One spring visit, as we pulled into our driveway, she remarked on the azaleas and dogwoods, reds and pinks and whites, brightened by the green zoysia and tree leaves. She sat between my sister and me in the back seat, and I tried to move a little away from her as she spoke. I nearly tumbled out after we parked. My father heaved her suitcase through the carport door, asked me to take it to the basement guest room, and disappeared into the kitchen. I stared at the dozen or so slate steps, then at the fat valise. The bag reached well past my waist. I hoisted it up against my hip with both hands and started down, my toes scouting ahead into the blind descent. Near the bottom I tripped, but I caught myself in time. Then I dragged the bag across the cement floor of the unfinished basement into the small guest bedroom. I turned to go back upstairs and almost ran into her in the doorway. She smiled and pressed a ten-dollar bill into my hand as I slipped past.

After getting settled, she brought a big white paper bag up to the kitchen.

"Well, what have we here?" my father asked, even though he had placed his order with her weeks before. He rubbed his hands together and chuckled. She reached into the bag, produced a gray cardboard box tied with red and white striped string, and set the box on the kitchen table.

"I cannot even tell you," she said, looking weary. "First I went to the Cakeland, then to Éclair. Agh!" She pursed her lips in frustration, then relaxed. "Kuglof," she announced, patting the package. She pulled out another box, this one smaller and rectangular. "And poppy seed cake."

"Good, very good!" my father exclaimed.

She produced a third box. "Cookies."

I leaned toward the cookie box as my father tugged at the knot and then began unraveling the endless length of baker's string. He opened it and revealed a dizzying pile of small, strange cookies — half-moon shapes, powder-coated round balls, thin circles topped with sprinkles or jam, wavy oblong objects. A dusty smell curled into my nose.

"Oh, good," I said, without much energy.

"Uh! So uncouth! Such a barbarian!" said my father, teasing me, but also a little hurt by my rejection of desserts he had devoured in his boyhood.

After dinner, my father and my grandmother deconstructed the strange cakes. I sat and listened, my hopes for a real dessert fading. They pulled apart the poppy seed cake and, as they ate, they critiqued the sweetness and quantity of the filling. Then they unrolled a slice of kuglof and evaluated its texture and the quality of the chocolate. They sounded like longtime fans hashing over the current players and coach of a once-great football team. To the young rooter, the team might have looked decent enough, yet to those who had been around in the glory years, who understood greatness, the present squad could not measure up. Though I had no interest in the cakes, their talk brought to mind my Redskins, who had just been to the Super Bowl, and I found myself siding naturally with my father and grandmother.

As their assessments, their passion, gained steam, talk turned to Cakeland, a Hungarian bakery in Queens where she had worked for a time.

"The kuglof, it was so flaky and delicate, like the air," said my grandmother, chewing rhythmically, an intense expression on her face. "And the poppy seed cake was sweet and stuffed so generously," she added, lingering on the last word. "We always used a little more poppy seed than the recipe." She laughed.

"Oh, yes, I remember," said my father.

Then her face turned dark. "Agh! The new owners, they cheapened the ingredients and made the filling so thin!" she said, her thumb and index finger pressed together, bitter at these crimes against proper pastry-making. Later, they retired to the living room and spoke in an odd duet, my grandmother in Hungarian, my father in English. I helped my mother clear the dishes, and afterward she sat me down with a Hostess cupcake and a glass of milk.

In 1991, at twenty-seven, I took a job in Connecticut, within reach of the city, and my father began to badger me about getting in touch with my grandmother. "Just a quick call," he noodged, or "Don't you go to New York ever?" I was living alone in a small town, and I went to New York for the warm companionship of old friends. My affection for my grandmother was lifeless, the residue in early adulthood of the habitual gestures of a child, and I had no interest in playing the dutiful grandson. It was difficult to picture what we would even do if we got together. I made excuses to my father and put him off. Still, in the way only parents can stimulate, a vague sense of guilt began building in the back of my mind until, on a particularly quiet fall evening, I phoned her. Just one call, I thought, there won't be anything more to it.

[3]

"Mr. Szabo!" said my father, waving me into the apartment. "Leave the door open." He was sitting in the living room making a list, and, as he rose and gave me one of his bear hugs, I noted that he looked better than I had expected. The mix of joy and sadness in his warm hazel eyes, which curved down ever so slightly at the corners, was balanced in favor of gladness. His joy was calm and heartfelt at times, manic at others. It was not yet clear which of these it was just now.

I glanced around. The apartment was dark, smelled stale, and felt cramped. Everything seemed on top of everything else. The front door opened directly into a living room, which adjoined a dining room. Right off the dining room was a tiny kitchen. The only sense of separateness lay at the back of the living room, where a slim hallway led to a bathroom and a study.

My Aunt Eve came over, reaching out her hand as she approached. She wore tight slacks and a sweater with a plunging neckline, and though her large breasts sagged and her hips broadened from a soft waistline, even nearing seventy she remained curvaceous. She had once been quite beautiful, sexy even, and she carried herself like a woman who knew it. "Thank you for coming, dear Peter," she said, kissing the air as she touched my cheek with hers.

My father and Eve returned to the list he had been making, and neither wanting nor receiving an immediate task, I drifted back to the study. On one wall of the small room was a collection of pictures, all men. There was my grandfather in his Austro-Hungarian military uniform, my grandmother's brother Pauli, the great composer Béla Bartok, and Oscar Kemeny. Kemeny had been my grandfather's business partner. Later he helped my grandmother arrange the escape from Hungary. I studied the photo. His intense gaze, busy eyebrows, and thick, tousled hair conveyed wildness and passion. Eve said he and my grandmother were lovers after the war. She made outlandish claims as often as she told difficult truths, and I did not know whether to believe her. Even so, something in the idea struck me as plausible. While it was hard to imagine my aged grandmother ever having been involved in a steamy romance, it was not far-fetched that a calculation of what Kemeny could do for her had produced a liaison. Whatever their relationship had been, it was significant, for here he was on the wall of her apartment fifty years after she left Hungary.

I went over to the study window, which opened to a miniature backyard. On childhood visits, my sister and I were told that the yard did not belong to my grandmother and we were not allowed to play there. As I scanned the high wooden fence that ringed the little lawn, a sudden desire to leave overcame me. The urge felt familiar, and I remembered how brief our few stops at the apartment were when I was young and how we never stayed overnight. Even in recent years, the several times I had come out to see her, I took her out to a nearby coffee shop or dropped her off after dinner. I did not dally. Why? I wondered. What was the source of this invisible pressure to depart that seemed to set in almost upon arrival?

For some reason, I thought of my father, and how in his late thirties he had decided to take up sailing. Charts of Chesapeake Bay soon covered his desk, and he pored over course books, with their odd nautical terminology and impossible knot diagrams. He bought a sailboat, and spring through fall we spent many weekends exploring the bay. Sometimes our destination was Annapolis for boating supplies and lunch at the market, where he would inhale a dozen fresh oysters and teach me how to pick blue crabs. Sometimes we headed for the Severn, or some other river, to anchor for the night. Those were pleasant evenings – family dinners and falling asleep to the gentle slapping of the water on the hull, the irregular, soft clang of main sheet on mast. One fall, my father and I took a trip, just the two of us. At the end of the first day, we moored next to a large cornfield, and when we awoke, a crowd of Canadian geese was breakfasting on harvest remains. We ate and readied ourselves in near silence, listening to their chatter. I pulled up the anchor and dunked it a few times to wash off the mud in the opaque, green-brown water. As I lifted it out, the chain rattled loudly against the pulpit and in an instant the hundred or so geese closest to us raised their heads and studied us. There was little wind, so we had no choice but to use the motor to get out to the river. My father fired up the outboard, and the massive flock issued a great honk of alarm and rose as one into the gray sky.

As we made our way back to Whitehall Bay later that afternoon, the western horizon darkened and the air grew moist. The wind stiffened and my father gave me the tiller, then he went below to listen to the latest weather report. The tiller struggled to pull itself from my grasp and turn the boat into the wind. I yanked back, jerked in the main sheet, and the boat heeled a bit more. The bow cut the water in stiff chops, the lines were tense, the sails full to bursting. I was in my early teens and I had grown to love speed in all forms. I turned my face into the wind and closed my eyes, listening to the vessel as it pounded its way through the water. When I opened my eyes, I was jolted by the threatening sky and hoped my father would return soon. He emerged from the cabin, glanced up, then at me. "Well, Mr. Szabo," he said zestfully, "looking like things are getting interesting. Would you mind if I took a turn at the helm, captain?"

He mastered anything that was a matter of learning skills, troubleshooting, or making a plan. He broke it down, tackled it step-by-step. But when the subject involved personal emotional difficulty, he became ignorant, distant, or belligerent. He loved easily, and when he expressed himself on most subjects, he did so without inhibition. Yet he also had a profound instinct to separate, to leave. On phone calls home, after offering a few highlights from his week, he would announce, "Well, that's all from Lake Wobegon," and leave me and my mother to finish the conversation. He said it in the friendliest of voices, but I felt pushed away. In those moments I experienced brief sensations of great sadness, sometimes in motion, like a riptide, sometimes fixed and pulling other things toward its mass. That I had an immediate desire to leave my grandmother's apartment, even when visiting there as an adult and without my father, suggested that some of this sadness had been imparted to me.

And what of my grandmother? She must have played a part as well in shaping what the apartment had come to mean. I gazed at the bright green grass out back, trying in vain to recall a meal cooked for us by my grandmother in her own home, a night of conversation and laughter and lingering.

"Well, let's get started," my father said with a sigh. Eve opened the hall closet, and I followed my father into the dining room where he began to set aside some of the valuables: a silver tabletop mirror, candlestick holders, a silver-plated serving platter, a tea set. Eve dumped an armful of clothes on the living room floor, starting a giveaway pile; I recognized the beige pantsuit my grandmother had worn to many of our lunches in the city.

Uncomfortable with the idea of riffling through her clothes and incapable of making judgments as to what things had monetary value, I sat down in front of a chest of drawers, pulled several photo albums from the bottom drawer, and started to flip through them. There were sunsets, page after page of them. Interspersed with sunsets were pictures of my grandmother with other short old ladies in front of apartment buildings and in dining rooms. These were her old friends, Hungarians mostly. They had a standing lunch date that rotated from one apartment to another, and each of them tried to outdo the last with how sharp her home looked, how nice the food was. On one page, she was pictured with several black women outside a plain building and at a restaurant. From their somewhat casual dress and friendly bearing, I guessed that they were her co-workers from her city government job. I put the albums back and opened the middle drawer. I grabbed a handful of envelopes and tossed them in a trash bag. Deeper in the drawer I found playing cards, decorative spoons, unused postcards, and notebooks from the Hunter College classes she audited, filled with her distinctive, meticulous cursive. It was like channel surfing – so many items, images, and different depths of meaning. I stood up, stretched, and stared at the empty wall in front of me for a minute. With declining energy, I returned to the chest. An old plastic bag was next to the Hunter notebooks. I removed it, gently pulled out a handful of worn, brown-edged papers, and began to leaf through them. They had the bold type, elaborate signatures, and stamps of official documents. I tried to decipher the Hungarian declarations. Then a voice inside reminded me there were only two days to get the job done, and I shook the papers back into the bag and placed it in the drawer.

A fog enveloped me. The objects in the chest, the old photos in the back room, the presence of my father and my aunt, just being there in that living room, produced a kind of narcotic cocktail in my brain. I became absorbed in the surreal environment of the apartment and disconnected from the concerns of my day-to-day life. I looked at my father, who was going through some silverware. "So what was your apartment like?" I said, a bit surprised by the question myself.

"What apartment?" he said, distracted.

"Budapest. The one in Budapest." I pictured old buildings and street cars.

"Budapest?"

I nodded.

"I don't remember," he said.

I felt deflated; my first instinct was to drop the matter. But then I grew annoyed. When my sister and I were younger, occasionally we would ask him about his youth in Hungary. We asked about his school, his summers, his father. Other than two or three brief and well-worn stories, his answer was always the same, "I don't remember." He offered details the few times he recounted their escape from Hungary. Beyond that, his past was blank. We continued asking anyway, though with declining frequency, as our efforts proved fruitless. Perhaps we persisted as long as we did because of the promise of hidden treasure suggested by the hesitancy in his voice, the lines of helplessness on his face that accompanied his empty replies. He seemed to know he should remember more, to sense there was a passage into his memory somewhere that he could not, or would not, find. Each time, pressing him only increased his distress, so by late childhood we withdrew.

But now his face remained relaxed, and he paused and thought for a moment. Instead of turning back to the silverware, he answered. "You came into the building through a door," he said, looking at me, then off into nothingness, "and it had a center like all European apartment buildings, oh God, a...."

"A courtyard?" I said, with encouragement.

"A courtyard, yes," said Eve from the hallway. "You came up the stairs to the apartment, a large apartment," she explained, walking into the room, several dresses slung over one elbow. "Kitchen, maid's room, pantry, past that was the dining room and living room. There was a study, the kids' room was in the corner, and then there was the parents' bedroom." She paused. "Do you follow?"

"Yes, yes," I said to her, trying to hold my father in the memory with my eyes, hoping he would fill the brief pause I had created. He had a fork in his hand, and he squinted at stacks of cutlery, searching for the right one to place it on.

"Each room had one of those beautiful heating stoves, with tiles," Eve said, opening a hand and waving it above her head, "and we heated with wood. But in our parents' bedroom, since my father was a prisoner of war in Siberia for five years after the First World War, he took the stove out. At bedtime he used to bring my mother heated bricks," she chuckled. "In the front there was a balcony. We lived on what they called the first floor, which is like the second floor here. There was a paint store underneath. Across the street there was a high school. Beautiful apartment, high ceilings, molding, everything."

She sat down next to me.

"That sounds comfortable," I said, giving in to the fact that she had wrestled control of the remembering from my father. "Your father must have been doing well."

"We had a hot water heater in the bathroom, which was very unusual," said Eve, touching her hand to her chest. "I never brag because, look, there's always somebody richer. There's only one person with nobody richer, Bill Gates. Why should I go around with my tongue hanging out being envious? I don't really care. Oh, I'd like to have more, but I don't. Boom. Finished. Right?"

"There's always someone," I said, trying to sound empathic.

"I don't know," said my father. My attention shot toward him. "I had a friend on the other side of Andrássy út, this big boulevard, kind of like Park Avenue. He lived in a villa. Now those people were well-to-do. We were comfortable, but middle-class, upper middle-class."

"Dani," said Eve, not conceding the point. "Remember the Italian school? My father said about us, 'They already speak two languages, let them go to Italian school.' Soon as I walked in, I had to learn reading, writing, arithmetic in Italian. That is why my mind is so well-exercised. European education is very good. You can check that. You'll see," she said, leaning toward me from the edge of her seat. I felt apologetic, though I did not know for what.

"And there was a maid and a lady who washed the clothes," she continued, pointing at me, "and a girl who came after school and took us to the Városliget. You know the Városliget?"

"No," I said.

"That is the main park in Budapest. A *big* park," she said, getting up and returning to the hallway. "And in the wintertime it had a skating rink where I used to figure skate. It was wonderful." She disappeared into the bathroom, and it was quiet for a minute. I opened the top drawer of the chest and started to rummage through it.

"In the front of the building there was a tiny fenced-in garden with a little sandbox," my father said, his eyes squinting as if he were squeezing out the memories like the last drops from a lemon. "I had a friend, we used to play there." He smiled, then went back to work on the silverware.

I imagined the two boys, playing tag and hide-and-seek on summer nights, as I had. I watched as they walked to the friend's house, crossing the boulevard and then arriving at the villa. It appeared in my mind as a large, elegant, three-story structure surrounded by a high wrought-iron fence and tall trees. A path led through a garden to the front door. A maid showed them in. The boys played board games and marbles in a parlor filled with antiques and velvet. Late in the afternoon they were served tea and cakes. They laughed at jokes I could not hear, their faces smeared with chocolate and jam, their button shirts stained with tea.

"Ugh!" said Eve, frowning as she came into the living room. "After you called me that morning to tell me she didn't sound so good," she said to my father, "I tried several times, then I called Irene and told her to go over to the apartment. You know Emery's sister, Irene?" she said to me.

I nodded.

"When Irene got there, she was on the floor, couldn't move." Eve lifted her index finger and the rag-like cloth that hung from it. "She had soiled herself." A mix of sadness and boredom circled her eyes, and something resembling the start of a smile pushed at her cheeks. "Irene cleaned her up and changed her while they waited for the ambulance."

The gray rag dangled from Eve's finger, stiff and twisted, holding the shape it obtained after Irene had rinsed it, wrung it, and placed it on the towel bar to dry. Why even bother to wash it, I thought, as I noticed the elastic of the waistband. Then I blinked hard. Eve dropped the underwear into a large trash bag and went back to the hallway, only to return an instant later.

"Dani, Dani, look here!" she said, and I winced at the idea of what else she might have discovered. "Fur coats." She held a white one by the collar. "Not real though. Maybe Janet is interested, I don't know," Eve said, referring to one of her daughters as she stroked the sleeve. "I have some friends, too, who might be."

My father nodded, and then wrote "Furs, fake" and "Janet" on the list of my grandmother's possessions that were to be divided up or given away. I peered over his shoulder at the list. The sofa, the television, a few china items, a silver-plated mirror, a couple of old paintings, an antique chair. Barely two-thirds of a page was filled, and I was struck by how few things of even modest value she had accumulated over a very long life.

"What about the desk?" said my father, motioning with a pen in the direction of a small antique writing desk, a stout yet graceful box perched atop thin, knobby legs. The dark wood was warm with age. The top folded open into a writing surface. It had arrived back in the early 1970s, upon the death of the last surviving sister-in-law from her first marriage. I remembered the day my father's portion of the inheritance was delivered. I was about nine or ten years old. A large truck pulled into the driveway and unloaded two rough-hewn wooden crates in front of the carport. The driver pried the crates open so my father could verify the contents. As the truck had parked in the middle of what was also my basketball court, I stopped playing and came over to watch. My father pulled out the straw filling and bent into each of the crates. Then he signed some papers and watched the truck as it backed down the driveway. Answering my look, he told me the boxes contained a pair of antique chairs, a table, some china, and a number of other things. He said they had come from Hungary. I was not sure where Hungary was.

"From my aunt Bözsi. Elizabeth," he said.

"Your aunt?" I asked, surprised that we had relatives in Hungary. "Why did this come to us?"

"They had no children. None of them did. We are the only ones left," he said, in a tone that was pleasant, yet final.

I peered into the crates. The chairs looked fancy, not like something I would use. Then I dribbled off toward the basket.

My grandmother's desk must have come in a similar crate. Though it was a delicate antique, she used it every day. When we visited, the top was always open, her papers, bills, and an address book on the writing surface. The golden brown, other-worldly shimmer about the desk was as much a product of the spirit she had imparted to it as the aged grain of the wood.

"Arthur's interested," Eve said, referring to her antiques dealer friend who had been through the apartment a day or two earlier. I glanced back at the list in my father's hand. Arthur's name hovered next to several items. The desk was not yet one of them.

[4]

Three weeks after my guilt-driven phone call, I met my grandmother at Lincoln Center. I came in from Connecticut the night before, stayed up late dining and talking, crashed on a friend's futon, and slept in. People started calling, a brunch arrangement formed. I excused myself at the last possible moment, after having made plans to meet up for dinner and then go to a party downtown. From the subway, I walked to the plaza, entering from the north side, by the Juilliard School. I stopped to take in the sun-brightened white marble landscape. Early arrivals for the Met matinee made a straight line from their taxis on Columbus Avenue to the tall arches of the opera, while others crossed diagonally toward me and the theater or toward the other side of the Met. At the center of the plaza churned the great fountain, a geyser-like jet ringed by smaller streams of water. The fountain muffled all other sound with a loud and constant *Shhhh*! I watched the water from the main spigot shoot straight and high into the air, then fall back into the pool, and I wondered whether the water caused the noise more as it emerged from the pipes or more as it struck the surface of the pool.

I shaded my eyes with my hand and soon found my grandmother. Among the forms of the people traversing the plaza or gathered around the fountain, the short, thin lines of the children, round tourists, angular regulars, she was easy to spot. Like a wedge, her body thickened from her narrow feet to her solid waist. A stone block of a torso sat atop the wedge, uniformly bulky, but not fat, the only curve at the upper back, the accrued effect of geologic-like forces working on a life over eighty-seven years.

"Dear Peter," she said plaintively, turning her palms up, her face alive. "I have been here nearly half an hour." She laughed, and I could not tell if she was angry at me or embarrassed at having complained.

"I thought we said eleven?" I said in my defense.

"Yes, yes, we did. I am so happy to see you, dear," she said, her eyes aglow.

Her face was round, with a slightly hooked nose and a small mouth at its center, a sturdy chin anchoring its base. Her cheeks were pink and her skin shiny and taut. Her hair was short and blond or, rather, her wig was. The way she moved the bangs to the side with her fingers suggested that she believed it was her real hair. Despite its evident falseness, the wig bolstered an impression of her as confident and not old.

She buttoned her raincoat as she asked about my trip in to the city and started walking to the restaurant. At Columbus Avenue she put her hand on my elbow. It was an understandable action on her part – she needed to be able to steady herself if she stumbled – but, nevertheless, I pulled my arm in toward my body the tiniest bit, unready or disinclined to provide support, though she did not let go. As we approached the corner, I sensed a trace of affection in her grip and here, too, had the instinct to distance myself, to maintain isolation. My grandmother seemed to notice neither of these reactions, but I glanced around at the people seated on benches in the small slice of a park we passed through for reactions to my obvious discomfort. I thought I caught a knowing smirk on the faces of a couple of guys about my age. There was definite disapproval in the eyes of a group of middle-aged women, who I imagined thought me insufficiently devoted.

When we got the "Walk" signal to cross at Broadway, she let go and we stepped into the street. My pace quickened with relief, and I was past the median before she reached it. By that time the "Don't Walk" was flashing. She trudged forward. I grew nervous that she might not make it in time and cause a commotion or an accident. I stopped in the middle of the street, hoping my presence might draw her across. I thought about telling her to wait in the median, but instead said nothing. She looked straight ahead, oblivious, and my eyes darted from the waiting cars, to her, then back to the cars. The "Don't Walk" stopped flashing, the light turned yellow, and I knew only a few seconds remained. I gestured at her to hurry. She gazed at me blankly. A few feet from the curb she took my arm. I heard cabs accelerate past as we stepped onto the sidewalk.

She tugged me to Josephina, and a hostess showed us to a table in the back. I scanned the menu and decided. She studied it at length, her face hidden behind the large plastic bi-fold menu. I tapped my foot arrhythmically and noticed the rear garden. Was she asleep? I wondered. I remembered that she had recently returned from a visit to Hungary and I asked her about it.

"It was wonderful," she said, her eyes wide as she lowered the menu. "The sanatorium."

"Sanitarium?" I said. You mean, for crazy people? I thought.

She put down the knife she was using to butter her roll. "*Nem.* No, dear," she said. "Sanatorium. That is for the cure, for health." She raised and lowered her arms, bent and straightened them, and wriggled her wrists. "For the joints, the circulatory," she said. Then she touched her cheek and neck, "for the skin, the nervous system, glands. For the heart," she concluded, patting her chest as she returned to her bread. "Every day there are baths in the special mineral water that is from under Budapest. There is mud, massage, and the physical therapy. The doctors are wonderful."

Her trips to Hungary were an annual ritual, but I knew little more about them than the fact that she went. The sanatorium sounded part hospital, part resort, and I found it difficult to picture the combination. If she had real health problems, why not see a doctor? And if she did not, why not go to a beach? My father prepared her taxes, and I recalled a battle he once had on her behalf with the Internal Revenue Service over the deduction she had taken for the cost of a visit to Hungary. Though he won the argument on the grounds that it was a medical expense, the whole thing still felt foreign and a bit shady.

"And I saw my old friends and Eva. You know Eva?"

"Of course," I said, though I had only a vague recollection of my distant Hungarian cousin.

"And we went to the opera, several times. *La Forza del Destino.* Wonderful. Have you seen this?"

I shook my head. My ignorance of opera was complete.

"Agh," she said, with a sour frown. "That is Verdi," she continued, her face bright as a firework as she said his name. "The brother stabbing Leonora at the end, just when the lover discovers her. Just then." She paused, looking distraught. "So terrible." Then, oddly, she smiled. "It was beautiful."

I imagined the scene, a bit dizzied by her extreme and contradictory reactions. A knife, voices rising in desperate melodies, wretched cries of sadness. She seemed comfortable, at home even, with melodrama.

"And Eva?" I said, hoping to change the subject.

Her shoulders slumped. "Not so good. Life in Hungary is terrible. Terrible!" she said, hammering the first syllable. "Everything is so expensive now, and Eva has only a small pension. Her son, András, is not well, and Szuzi – that is the daughter – is very sick."

More tragedy. I realized how deep her particular fondness for it was. As she raved and pouted, the extremes of her opera-tinted view of life unsettled and exhausted me. She sighed. "There are so many political parties, like before the war. Some of them are anti-Semitic," she added with a knowing nod.

I did not know what else to say and let the conversation lapse. I checked my watch and thought about the party an old college friend was giving that night. The food arrived, and I was grateful. She ate with a gusto that approached coarseness. She chewed her chicken with large, circular motions of her jaw and gripped her knife and fork like weapons, holding them upright, fists resting on the table when she was not carving herself another bite. I thought about the sanatorium and the mineral baths as I watched her tear a hunk of bread and use it to pin down a chunk of meat so she could stab it with her fork. I thought about her vast knowledge of opera, her innumerable visits to museums. There was an earthiness to her, a trace of barbarism, along with the culture. It was a strange mix. I was halfway through my burger before I realized how long I had been staring at her.

"So what else did you do?" I asked.

She looked up at me, her gaze unfocused.

"In Budapest," I said. "What else did you do on your trip to Budapest?"

"Oh!" She nodded eagerly. "Yes, we went to the theater, and to the museum, and to the Ruszwurm, that is a coffee house in the Buda hills," she said, gesturing upward and to her right with her knife. "I wanted to go to Balaton, the lake, but there was no time."

"Is it far from Budapest, Lake Balaton?" I said, glancing again at my watch.

"Not so far," she said. "We used to go there in summer when the children were very young."

She returned to the last of her food. I recalled a summer vacation to a lake in New Hampshire when I was young and the solitary, late afternoon kayak paddles along the marshy shoreline. "Who used to go there, to the lake?" I asked.

"I went with Dani and Eve. And there was a lady who helped us and she would come. There was a kind of a house, a cabin, near the lake. We took the train there. Sandi, that is Alexander, he would come on weekends, and then for a few weeks."

Alexander was my grandfather. He died decades earlier, and the rare mention of his name engaged my attention. "That sounds nice," I said, starting to hope she might volunteer more.

She mopped her lips with her napkin, then pushed her empty plate away from her. "Tell me, dear Peter," she said, leaning forward, "how are you?"

I frowned, but she did not seem to notice.

"Well, I'm okay," I said. "I'm feeling a little restless, though."

"Oh?" she said, as she stirred her coffee, sensing melodrama.

I hesitated, not sure I wanted to say more, anxious about what she might relate back to my parents. But then, I decided to chance it.

"The man I am working for, the head of the agency, is an old family friend, and he says it's important to be sure you have played out an experience before leaving it. But I feel played out, you know, done with what I think I can do there. It's just not that interesting anymore."

I was not sure why I was telling my grandmother all this, and it felt a little odd. Yet as I spoke, her attention remained fixed on me, her expression open, receptive. As she listened without judgment, I felt relaxed in a way I had not for some time.

"I'm pretty young compared to everyone else there," I continued. "I live alone. It's funny, I find I don't mind that so much. But I would like to see people more. Friends. My parents are real proud of my job. That's good, anyway."

She did not respond for minute. She just nodded. Then she said, "It is a good job, dear. Important. But if you feel that you are finished," she said, spreading her hands, "what will you do?" She rubbed the tablecloth with the tips of her fingers.

I shrugged. "I am taking a few weeks off to think about it. Maybe come look for work in New York."

She nodded, but she gave no hint of excitement that I might end up close by.

"Something different." I tried to sound unconcerned, to hide the thinness of my convictions.

"And Norah? How is she?" she said.

I was still thinking about my work dilemma and trying to fight back familiar feelings of directionlessness, so the abrupt change of topic caught me by surprise. I did not respond at first. There had been enough sharing for one day, I thought, much more than I expected. But she had met Norah at graduation from graduate school, and maybe on one or two other occasions, so I felt she deserved an answer.

"We're not seeing each other right now," I said, before a sip of tea. "A couple of people I know saw her recently. I think she is all right," I added flatly, trying to discourage discussion.

She fixed her marble gray eyes on mine. "What is the matter, dear? She is a nice girl."

I grasped for a response that might explain the on-and-off relationship in a way that would also close off the topic. "I don't know," I said, looking away. "You know she is not Jewish?" As soon as I said it, it struck me as an odd thing to say to her. The words brought into relief my grandmother's a-religiousness. I could not recall a memory of her around a Seder table. It seemed impossible that she might speak Hebrew, or even Yiddish. She never mentioned going to synagogue and did not belong to one. The few special meals she made or treats she offered were Hungarian, not Jewish. Then, in my grandmother's gaze, I questioned myself. How much did it really even matter to me, Norah's religion? It began to feel like an excuse, more reflexive refuge than felt principle.

My grandmother nodded and shrugged, and there was a long pause during which she seemed to want to say something, but instead she sipped the last of her cool coffee.

"Tell me, dear," she said, wiping her mouth and putting her napkin on her plate, "do you want to be late to the opera?"

[5]

The desk safe for the moment, I turned to the wall of photographs and paintings behind the living room couch. A pair of portraits near the top caught my eye. On the left was my grandmother at middle age; on the right, her second husband, Emery. My grandmother was drawn in shades of gray, with pink and peach highlights on the forehead and cheeks. The artist had used pastel, and my grandmother's features were soft yet vibrant. It dawned on me that the picture would be nice to have, and I began to imagine where I might hang it in my small apartment.

"That's a beautiful painting of her," I said to my aunt, who had joined me. "I like the colors and the expression on her face."

"We've sold this one," Eve said, aiming her finger at Emery, "and I am taking Granny."

I feigned indifference. "And who are these people?" I asked, pointing to a black-and-white picture of a group of well-dressed people in what looked like a living room. A man and two women were seated in chairs. Two couples stood behind them. The men wore suits and confident expressions, the women, simple, tight dresses and hats that hugged their faces. Their clothes suggested the 1920s, the furniture and the paintings in the background, at least modest wealth.

"That is Granny and Sandi, or Alexander, as you might say," Eve said, tapping my grandmother and grandfather. I leaned closer and studied the seated couple. We did not have any pictures of my Hungarian grandparents in the house growing up. The only old photograph we had of either of them captured my grandfather in his World War I, Austro-Hungarian military uniform. But that was long before they were married. I recognized my father instantly in the bald, round-faced man in the picture now before me. There were differences, chiefly a regal bearing in my grandfather that was distinct from my father, the impression aided by his trim mustache, his starched collar, and his bored-yet-engaged expression. Even so, there was the same kindness at the edges of his eyes. My grandmother had talked about him during our meetings in the city, but seeing an image of him was somehow more captivating, although perhaps it was her stories that fueled the captivation.

"The women, those are Sandi's three sisters," Eve said, a smile spreading across her face. "Margaret, Erzébeth, or Bözsi as we called her, and Jancsi. My father used to tease them mercilessly when they were children."

I pictured a boy in woolen knickers and stiff shoes chasing three girls. He laughed as they glanced back and shrieked at the spider he had jarred and then held in his outstretched hand.

"The seated one, that is Jancsi," Eve continued. "How I adored her!"

"Tall, drawn, very sad person," said my father, who now stood beside us.

I looked at Jancsi. Her long limbs confirmed a certain lankiness, and her hat was pulled down toward her eyes.

"She kept her apartment dark. There was a samovar, and all day long she drank this dark black tea." He wrinkled his nose as if he had just sipped the harsh liquid. "Very pessimistic."

"Well, she became a widow in the First World War," Eve said feistily, "the very first day. And then the same year her baby was stillborn. So you can understand why she would be bitter."

I nodded, but my father just stared at the picture, not hearing her. "When we had to move into a Jewish building during the war," he said, "Jancsi and Bözsi lived on the same floor."

He went on, but he was drowned out in my mind by the echo of two of the words he had just said, "Jewish building." No one in my family ever discussed the war when I was growing up. Much later, during one of my visits with her, my grandmother had talked about having to hide after the Nazis occupied Budapest. But the way she told it, it seemed as if everyone hid, not just Jews. I had not made a conscious connection between my father, my grandmother, and my aunt and the threats they endured because they were Jewish. I knew my father was a Jew. I knew he had lived in Hungary during the war. But somehow this knowledge remained vague and semiconscious. It was as if a concrete barrier existed between what had taken place and what I understood. I sensed how long that barrier had been in place. To be sure, cracks had emerged, especially after the visits with my grandmother started. Now, "Jewish building" struck as a blow to the barrier, the cracks lengthened and deepened, and a kind of dark and familiar excitement welled up. I looked at my father intently, hoping for more, but he and Eve were still concentrating on the photograph.

"Dani was Bözsi's favorite," Eve said. "She married Miklós, that is Michael in English, only he was more a Miklós than a Michael." She giggled as she pointed at one of the standing men, but she offered nothing to explain the difference. "His brother was Lendyl Auriel; his family owned more than two dozen apartment buildings in the city. That was one of their buildings."

I remembered the crate we had received years earlier, and the inheritance within.

"What was?" I asked, thinking at first she meant the apartment in which the photograph was taken.

"The building we had to move to in the war."

"So they were Jews, the Auriels?" I said.

"The Lendyls," she corrected. "In Hungary we say the last name first. Lendyl Auriel is like Smith John here, which is John Smith. Yes, they were Jews."

My father stared at the picture. "Our apartment was in the middle," he said. "Bözsi was to the left, and Jancsi was on the other side."

I imagined an open, square corridor ringing a courtyard several stories below, heard a distant click of footsteps on tile, wondered whether Jancsi had brought the samovar with her to the Jewish building. I hungered for details about the place so I could picture more of the experiences. Yet it was a different sort of question that my mouth formed. "You all were in a Jewish building? During the war?"

"Yes," my father said. "My aunts were converted to Catholicism for many years, so though they moved there with us, they were sort of exempt."

My grandmother had told me about the three converted sisters. Until now, they appeared in my mind as stone-carved figures aligned in a row above a cathedral entrance.

"Bözsi was one of the few people who had an electric refrigerator," my father continued. "Most Jews could not have them. Or maybe it was because they were well off." He paused and frowned. "I think one of them knew Szálasi or had a friend that knew him. That got them some protection."

"Szálasi?" I said. He sounded important, probably some well-connected Jewish official, I thought.

"The Hungarian Nazi leader," he said.

Confusion set in. I wanted time to sort it out. But the little my father had just recounted about the war and his family was much more than he ever had said. I did not want to lose the moment. So I pressed on.

"Bözsi's husband, Miklós, was he around?" I asked.

"Before the war Uncle Miklós was a banker," said my father. "His family left for England in the late 1930s and he administered the family's businesses." He looked down at his hands, then at me. "Then he was taken for labor service. My uncle Pauli, many Jews were. All the shit work for the army. Very harsh."

He sighed and smiled. "My father died in 1943. After the war, Miklós, he was my father figure. He would take me to Gerbeaud, a patisserie on a lovely square in Pest. We would sit at a table outside. I remember there was a special flaky pastry stuffed with chestnut that I loved." The thought of it filled him with child-like excitement. "Uh! Nothing like that here.

"I was twelve, thirteen, fourteen. He asked me about school. I think maybe we talked about my father, things I wanted to do; later, girls. We would go in the afternoon, after school. It was filled with people having coffee, the square was busy. Then he would walk me home."

I saw them as if from a nearby table. Miklós was well-dressed, portly, with a bushy mustache flanked by fleshy cheeks, dark eyes. My father shifted in his seat, school bag by his feet, his face serious. People bustled through the square on their way home from work. Masons knocked off for the day, stones and bags of cement piled high in front of the old buildings they were reconstructing. A crowd of college-age young people strolled by, laughing and arguing. From one of the side streets, the bell of a streetcar echoed. Miklós had no children of his own and the lines of his brow and his soft eyes conveyed both a sense of responsibility and a liking for his nephew. And there was my father, and I identified with his adolescent intensity and conflicts. He leaned into the table, grateful for his uncle's attention and advice. But there was something in the way he glanced at his shoes from time to time that hinted at a struggle I did not share at that age: how incomplete had been the mourning, how much his father's absence must have meant.

My father stood and lifted the picture from its hook. "God," he said. He tapped a finger on the third woman and the man next to her. "Margaret and her husband, Steiner Sándor. When I was a boy, my parents used to send me to their house to fatten me up. So they succeeded, finally," he said with a laugh as he patted his large belly. "They had a place in Buda. You took a streetcar to the end of the line, and then you walked through this beautiful neighborhood of villas up a hill to the top. In front of the house was this gradually rising area, with a walk in the middle and fruit trees on either side. Gorgeous roses. Behind the house there was a steep hill where they grew grapes. I remember I had a friend who was a peasant boy. I must have been six or seven." He shook his head and smiled. "On walks from the streetcar, I would pass this Hungarian sheep dog, a black dog with hair covering the eyes. I kept asking my aunt and uncle, 'How does this dog move around if it can't see?'" he said with exaggerated innocence. "My uncle told me it was not a real dog, it was mechanical, got wound up every morning." He chuckled with delight and I laughed with him. "I was so gullible, I believed them. Every time I passed the dog I looked at it and thought, 'This is a toy dog, how incredible!'" he said, mimicking his mistaken awe. He was a savvy man, but there was also a naiveté about him that was easy to trace back to the boy filled with wonder as he stared at the would-be mechanical dog.

"The husband, my uncle Sándor, he was taken away to labor service and never returned," he said, his tone matter-of-fact. "Very nice man." He set the picture down on top of the television. "They had a daughter, Maritza. She ran a Montessori kindergarten in their apartment in Pest, I think," he said, stepping into the kitchen to get a drink.

I wanted to follow him, to hear and to see more, but as I made to do so, Eve spoke.

"Maritza had a lover after the war," she said, sorting plates at the dining table. "He was a married man. Something happened to end it and she threw herself in front of a streetcar. Killed herself. Poor girl." I waited for her to go on, but she picked up a stack of china plates and said loudly to the kitchen, "Dani, where do you want to put these?"

He glanced through the doorway. "Oh, on the table," he said in between gulps of water. "The table is fine."

[6]

I called her over Christmas to say a quick hello, but gave her no openings to make a plan to get together. Things got busy at work, then winter set in, and I did not travel in to New York. I had changed apartments back in the fall, trying to save on rent, moving from a one bedroom in an apartment building on the main drag to a place on a quiet side street. The new building had four units, one on each floor. It was old and more than a little run-down. The building had a name, Hy-up, written in concrete on the side of the structure. The ground floor was occupied by a young couple who fought late into the night. One day they were evicted by force. The owner lived on the top floor. He had a glass eye, the result of a bad motorcycle accident, was often a little drunk, and had a shotgun in the corner of the main room of his place. He was gruff, but he took a liking to me, and sometimes, to break up a long, quiet weekend, I stopped up to say hello. The wattage was low, the floors creaky, and the wooden staircase that led from the outside to my third floor entrance groaned from the effort of holding me up. But the view offered a measure of relief. The building was set into a hillside, and I spent many evenings in a chair in my bedroom, looking out over athletic fields, past the juvenile detention center, to the forest in the distance.

The snow seemed to obscure everything but long days at work and evenings in that chair looking out at the purple-white view. In mid-March the snow turned to slush and soon vanished, and the soft, muddy ground released the first scents of spring. I bought a motorcycle and every day took the long way home from work. I made plans to visit friends in the city. As the weekend approached, the guilt at not having been in touch with my grandmother gained strength, and when a friend fell ill, opening Saturday afternoon, I phoned her. We met again at Josephina; a busy weekend crowd filled the place with noisy chatter. A peach-colored glow spread across her face when she saw me, and as we sat down, she pulled a notebook from her bag.

"I have a class at the Hunter College, it is about Chinese history, so interesting." She gave her index finger a lick and flipped through the pages. "Ah, here it is. The Emperor Qin, he was the first emperor of China," she said, glancing at her notes. "When he died around 200 BC, he was buried with an army of eight thousand soldiers. They were made from terra-cotta, by hand, by seven hundred thousand workers. Can you believe it?" She stutter-stepped over the words.

"Some say the workers were buried alive so they would not tell secrets of the treasure in his tomb. Terrible! He wanted to take the army with him to conquer heaven!" She swayed side to side as she slapped her cheek in disbelief. "*Jaj, istenem!*"

I chuckled, more as a defense against her overwhelming enthusiasm, her sincerity, than as an affirmation.

She browsed ahead a few pages. "Here, ah," and she began telling me how Emperor Qin had started the Great Wall and the civil service. She recounted the high stakes around the grueling Chinese civil service exam, and the preparations people went through. "It was maybe one in a hundred who passed," she said. "Only the test mattered, not your family or who it was that you knew. This was a real meritocracy. Fifteen hundred years ago. Can you imagine?"

"It is pretty incredible," I said, surrendering to her sense of wonder. "You think how long ago that was, and how far along they were."

"The professor is wonderful, so smart, very handsome," she said, blushing a little.

Lunch arrived and she put the notebook away.

"Tell me dear Peter, so what else is new?"

I was uncomfortable with how much I had volunteered about my life and worries during our initial visit, and I had vowed to keep things more removed and formal if I ever met with her again. She was my grandmother, after all, not a friend, I told myself. But in the months that followed our first meeting, I found myself thinking about her. It was only a brief moment here and there, but the fleeting recollections stirred feelings of calmness and safety. "Well," I said.

"Yes?" She bent forward.

"I bought a motorcycle."

"A motorcycle!" she said, almost shouting.

Relieved she had not scolded me, I spilled details. "It's a black Yamaha Maxim 650. I took a safety class before I got it, and I've put a ton of miles on it over the last month. Though I have to tell you, as I was riding home after I picked it up, I said to myself, 'What the hell are you doing on a motorcycle!'" I laughed, my body shook, and my smile stretched long-stiff muscles in my face.

"You know," she said nodding and glancing at the tables on either side of us, "I rode on a motorcycle once."

I was startled. "No, really?"

"I was a young girl, maybe fifteen," she said in a low voice. "I was visiting my cousins Simon and István in the countryside. After I got there, Simon, he was my favorite, he said to me, 'Maria, come outside, I want to show you my new horse.' I expected a horse, you know, big, and with a tail." She shook her head. "*Nem*, this horse was a motorcycle, and it had a thing for someone else to sit in." She swept her hand back and forth next to her chair.

"You mean a side car?" I said.

"Yes, a side car, and he asked me, 'Would you like to go for a ride?' I told him, joking, 'Only if you know what you are doing!'"

I pictured the motorcycle and side car, but had difficulty forming a mental image of her as a young woman.

"So, anyway, he went inside and brought back another pair of goggles. Then he started the motorcycle and I got in." She moved her hands from her forehead down to her eyes, as if she were putting on the goggles. "Everyone came out into the yard, and they waved as we left. It was very loud as Simon drove through the town. People were looking out their windows at the noise. Then we were out in the countryside." She closed her eyes and shook her head. "It was a beautiful day. Beautiful. He said something to me but I could not hear, I did not care, it was so fast, so wonderful."

I thought about my motorcycle, the hiss of the air rushing through my helmet, the force of the wind against my chest, the husky hum of the engine, the euphoria of flight.

"Simon turned around in a field, and as we went back, he showed me how much faster it could go."

I nodded, understanding how tempting the twist of the throttle could be.

"Just before the town there was a curve in the road. He was going so fast, my God!" she said, rocking her head back and forth. "We went off the road and the whole motorcycle rolled over three, maybe four times. The neighbors all ran to us, then they carried me back to my cousin's house. I was in bed for two weeks!" she said, her shoulders shaking with laughter, her face turning bright red. "*Jaj*, it was terrible!"

I worried about her injuries, but I identified with the profound thrill of her experience, with her exuberance, and I laughed, too. "Well, I don't have a side car," I said, leaning toward her and lowering my voice, "but if I get one...." And she chuckled some more.

After lunch we walked up the block to the movie theater at Lincoln Plaza to see *The Piano*. The theater was packed, but somehow we found two seats in the middle. Shortly after the lights went down, I heard the loud crinkling of cellophane as my grandmother unwrapped a sucking candy to calm her chronic cough. Someone shushed. A little while later, I looked over, and she was asleep. In a few more minutes, she started to snore. I heard a few sighs from people around us, and I poked her with my elbow. Her head bobbed up and her eyes opened.

"What did he say?" she said.

"He's asking about the piano," I whispered, aware of the dozen or so pairs of eyes upon us. "He wants lessons."

"Oh," she said and was dozing an instant later. I refined my nudge so that each time she started to snore, I touched her hard enough to stop the noise, but gently enough so that I did not wake her. Once I glanced over to see her sitting wide-eyed, mouth open, staring at Harvey Keitel and Holly Hunter both naked, clenched together. I looked back at the screen and grew hot with embarrassment. Soon I heard snoring again.

When the movie ended, I offered to accompany her to the subway. We walked down Central Park West. In the park, new-green leaves shivered in a slight breeze and daffodils withered in shady glades. My grandmother held my arm with her hand. We were both quiet, but a certain intensity in her grip, in her pace, suggested she was reflecting on something.

"My first husband, your grandfather, he was a wonderful man and I loved him very much," she said, though from her gaze it was not clear that she was aware she was saying this aloud. "He managed a factory where they made shirts and suits. I was a secretary in the factory. After several months at the job, I was transferred to the director's office. Sándor, that is Alexander, was deputy director of the factory, and the job was in his office."

I walked evenly, like a bird watcher, careful not to disturb her.

"Then I was moved to the purchasing department, and the next day there was a note from him inviting me to dinner." She looked around. Tourists and young lovers were gathered around the monument at the southwest corner of Central Park, stretched out on its slender stone steps. "For six months we went to restaurants, to the opera. We picnicked on Margaret Island. One afternoon we went to Buda, to the hills. We walked along the Fisherman's Walk and looked at the city below. You know the Fisherman's Walk?" she asked.

I mouthed a silent no and shook my head.

"He told me the company was going to send him to Brussels to run their business there. Then we went to the Ruszwurm — that is the coffee house — and that is where he asked me to marry him."

She sat down on a bench, I joined her, and we stared out at Columbus Circle.

"Brussels was wonderful. I went to museums. I studied French. I promised him I would learn French, but I was never fluent," she said, looking repentant. "On weekends we went to Paris, to Amsterdam, to Germany. It was a year I will never forget, never."

She tightened the knot on her kerchief.

"Then he was transferred to run a factory in Prostějov, Prosnitz, whatever the Czechs call it, in Czechoslovakia. Finally, we moved back to Hungary. I took classes in cutting and sewing, and I began to teach sewing from home. He started his own business, wholesale fabrics. They sold fine material and denim, which had become very popular." Though she still looked at the traffic circle, she tilted her head toward me and nodded meaningfully. "Even during the war they were in business."

A flock of pigeons circled the monument.

"Every morning I would prepare for him three cigars. Then, in the store, sixty cigarettes he smoked. Sixty cigarettes," she said, frowning and holding up three fingers. "The first time he just blacked out, and they found him at his desk. At the hospital, the doctor told him to stop smoking, and he did. But it was too late. Two months later a cousin stopped by the store, a good customer, and they were telling jokes to each other. In the middle of a sentence he fainted. At the hospital the doctor met me outside the room and told me it was a massive brain hemorrhage. There was nothing they could do. He was dead."

We watched the scene by the monument. After a few minutes, she stood up, brushed her coat, and adjusted her kerchief. The sun peeked at us from behind the buildings across the circle, and the long, web-like shadows of the trees reached deep into the park. I did not know what to say. Sorry did not seem quite right – to a friend perhaps, but not to a grandmother. She smiled at me. "The R train is at Fifty-Seventh Street," she said. "Come." Then she picked up her bag and began walking east.

[7]

I glanced at the clock above the kitchen doorway, then around at the apartment. Midmorning already and it seemed as if we had barely touched the place. I knew I needed to dive into the cleanout, but the scent of the past hung in the room, and I hungered for more. I thought of the few anecdotes my father had offered in my childhood, repeated so many times they had turned to plastic. There was the story about how Alexander made them eat their spinach at breakfast if they did not finish it at dinner, and the legend, from long before my father was born, about how his father's beloved German shepherd had survived a jump out of a second-story window to greet my grandfather upon his return from a prisoner-of-war camp in Siberia. I thought of the excitement these tidbits had aroused and how disappointed we were at his response of "I don't remember" when we asked for more. Even so, in my youth, I had been relatively indifferent to his claims of barren memory. As a teen, I grew angry at him, though I was frustrated more by the fact that I could not overcome his powers of denial than by unfulfilled desires for more information. As I went to the desk and began sorting the bills from the past week's mail, I was tempted to prompt him again but I was anxious about how far behind with the work we seemed, and I suppressed the urge. My father folded linens and organized them into piles as a meditative silence settled over things.

"I remember bombers, British bombers," he said, after a while. "Behind the big park near the apartment, the Városliget, there was a zoo. And behind that was a Shell Oil refinery. They were trying to bomb the refinery." He squinted. "Must have been 1942, because I remember my father was there."

It was like coming across a family of deer in the woods, the sudden appearance of the recollections. I thought they might flee with any sudden movement, so I kept my head down, my attention focused on the mail.

"Each of us had a suitcase, and I had a little steel helmet and an armband. The sirens rang and we all went downstairs to the basement—my father, my mother, my sister, and I. I remember that in the cellar there was a small, concrete-lined steel door to the outside, like a window, and I used to push it open and look out until I heard the planes."

He looked up, as if to the sky, and lifted his right hand. "When the bombs fell, it was like a giant banging on the roof of the building with a great log. Bummm!" he said, making a fist and pounding it into his palm. "Bummm! Bummm! The whole apartment house shook, and sometimes the lights went out and people put on flashlights. There were always stray bombs. One time they hit the high school across the street from us and nearly destroyed it."

"Were you scared?" I asked.

"Oh, no," he chuckled, "it was fun, a big game to me. How old was I in 1942, nine years old? I was a kid, I didn't know." He paused and seemed to be still gazing out of the small basement door. "After an air raid, I loved to go outside and collect bomb fragments."

Herendi china, collected over her many trips to Hungary, filled a hutch in one corner of the dining room. As my father and I carefully emptied vases and teacups from the cabinet, I noticed their decorations. They were covered with birds and flowers that seemed both familiar and also somehow strange and foreign. I picked up a vase and examined it. The muted, dark colors were mesmerizing against the white background. The images were neither realistic nor caricatures—there was both fact and fantasy. Though flat and layered, the forms somehow flowed. There was a blend to the design, both Western and Eastern, melodic and dissonant, that was different from the rational relationships in the art I identified with. I set the vase down on the table next to a number of ceramic bells my father had just removed from the hutch. I picked up one of the bells. It was lighter than I expected, and when I flicked my wrist, it sang a rich tenor. I tried the smallest one, a sweet soprano.

"There is a set of them. I think Julie would love them," said my aunt, referring to one of her daughters.

I had the strange sensation of having been caught shoplifting, and I set the bell down quickly and returned to the cabinet. A small plate displayed on a wooden stand on a high shelf caught my eye. I pulled it down and felt the unusual latticework that ringed the edge of the piece. In the middle of the dessert-size dish was a black and white photographic image of a woman. She had a slight hook to her nose, a rounded chin, and soft eyes and looked to be in her thirties. Her hair was neatly styled into a tight bun. A frilly white collar, bright and intricate, covered her neck. I guessed the image had been taken in the late nineteenth century or very early twentieth. The fact that the photograph was imprinted upon the plate indicated some means, but the woman wore no jewelry or other accessories.

"That is Julia, Granny's mother," said Eve, as she walked over. "Nice lady, quiet. Babushka-like. You know babushka?"

I nodded, but it was not easy to picture this pretty woman as an old babushka.

"She died a few years after we left." Eve picked up a companion plate from the shelf. "And this was Granny's father," she said. Like the other picture, he was only visible from the collar up, but it was still possible to see that he wore a jacket. His clothes were a sharp contrast—black suit and tie, white shirt. He had short dark hair and a full mustache. His blank eyes rested to the side of angular cheekbones. I noticed a large chip in the plate.

"Granny's family was from Herend and they knew the owners of the famous Herendi china company. The owners made these plates for them. Dani, how about I take Julia and you take him?" she said to my father, waving the plates at him. My father was in the living room and appeared not to hear her.

"Mor, that is her father, he abused Granny when she was a little girl, you know, touched her," Eve said to me, sounding unaffected. "I think that is why she loved men so much."

I frowned and wondered how Eve could know such a thing. It seemed unlikely that my grandmother had told her. I wanted to write it off as just another of her outrageous comments, but it was true that my grandmother's feelings for certain men — one or two of her Hunter professors, her brother, my father — were unusually strong. It occurred to me that I had experienced her intense affection as well. As I offered Eve a nod, I tried to hide my doubt and discomfort.

"My father used to put a board onto the bathtub and massage us with rubbing alcohol nearly every day," she said. "Me and Dani."

"Sort of a health thing?"

"He never touched me that way," she said, with a twitch of her head toward the man on the plate. "He loved me." Despair crossed her face, then a bright smile. "And we got cod liver oil every day." She chuckled. "You know how big the Hungarian soup spoons are?" She looked at me out of the corners of her eyes in a way that assured me that I did not. "I will never forget the yellow oil, with a little dab of jam right here on the end." She pointed to the spoon she pretended to hold in front of her mouth, and she laughed. "It was disgusting. But it was because he loved us."

I smiled, imagining the firmness and warmth of his touch.

"And when I got whooping cough, you know what my father did? He took me to the bus terminal to inhale bus fumes." Pleasure thinned her incredulity.

"Bus fumes?"

"It was an old wives' tale, but it worked!"

I became aware of the absence of my father from the conversation, and I turned to see what he was doing. The narrowing of his eyes and the absentminded way he stuffed clothes into one of the giveaway bags suggested he had been listening to us.

"How about you, Dad, what do you remember?" I said.

"About my father?" he said.

"Yes."

He shook his head. "The rubdowns, that's the only thing I remember, these alcohol rubdowns. Supposed to be good for children. But I really have no recollections."

He pushed a few more clothes into a bag, then he stopped.

"I remember the four of us at the dining table. He had high blood pressure and on the table there was always a bottle of this horrible artificial salt. Strange color. Tasted terrible." He scrunched his nose. "Nothing else," he said, his face flattening. "I don't remember." Then he fell silent and returned to the work.

I did not want him to stop. "What about his political beliefs?" I said, reaching for the first thing that came to my mind. "Was he patriotic or conservative or anything?"

"No, nothing, I don't remember," he said, without looking up. But as I turned back to the hutch, he went on.

"Well, my mother said they moved back from a job in Czechoslovakia because he wanted me to be born in Hungary." He tilted his head, eyebrows up. "So that was patriotic maybe." He stood up. "But you have to remember, when he was alive, I was ten years old. Do you expect to discuss your political beliefs with your ten-year-old son?"

"Well, it's different times," I said, shrugging.

He shook his head. "When I was a kid, the parents were up here," he said, poking the air above his head, "and you were a little worm. You did as you were told. The parents were loving, but authoritarian; there was no discussion. They said 'Do this,' and that's what you did. I have no recollection of his political beliefs, or religious beliefs, or anything," he said, agitated. "Nothing."

"We never went anywhere," Eve chimed in. "We lived in the *kindertsima*, the children's room. There was a great sense of hierarchy, of boundaries."

"In the family?" I said.

"Yes, which creates tremendous security, Peter darling." She found a chair, and sat down as she continued. "Lots of discipline, but no hitting, no yelling. One day, I remember cousin Eva coming over on a Sunday. She and I were playing in a room and making a lot of noise. My father just came to the doorway, stood there, and glared at us." She made a glowering face and then burst into giggles. "We stopped talking!" She slapped her knee and leaned toward me, pointing. "He would say to her parents, 'Let your kids come to the Szabo hell and I will teach you how to raise children.' These kids got chocolate. We had cod liver oil!" she said, her expression proud and loving.

"Granny, she was sort of a second-class citizen," she said. "She didn't have much say. My father had his concepts of how to raise children. Nobody in her family had been a prisoner of war in Siberia for five years like he had, with all that regimen. Right? It was different." She got up, and in the silence that followed, I watched as she examined the china on the dining table.

"He used to walk us to school every day on the way to his business," said my father.

I had been drawn in by Eve, and I tried to keep my expectations in check as I turned back toward him.

"Every day?" I said.

"Dani was vomiting every morning, did you know that?" said Eve, smirking.

I shook my head.

"I used to get nervous about going to school, I don't know why," said my father, embarrassed. "I would throw up in the street. Then my father would say, 'Okay, now go to school.'" He laughed. "Sometimes he took pity on me and he brought me back home."

"Then he was dead," said Eve.

My father looked at her, then me, and though he went on as if she had said nothing, I sensed his mood had changed. "At school, I'd always say to him, 'kiss good-bye' and he would kiss me good-bye," he said. "That day I remember was different. I said 'kiss good-bye' in the apartment, and we kissed good-bye there."

"Everything was regular," said Eve. "The maid was there, the girl came and took us to school, my mother went to her tailoring class." Her face grew pink. "When we got home, everybody was crying, and all we were told is that he died. We were not even allowed to the funeral." She wagged a finger at me. "While it was going on, we were home playing a table game in the nursery. I was confused. I was numb. I wanted to be there. But we were left here at the apartment playing a game."

"The family decided it was not good for us to go," my father said, his voice desperately empty of emotion.

I imagined two children in school clothes kneeling around a low table. A young woman pushes a pair of dice across a board to the boy. "Come, children," she says, trying to sound authoritative. "Play." The boy picks up the dice and drops them weakly. The girl's eyes are red and wet. The boy's face is white. The sound of a ticking clock drifts in from the hallway. Someone has draped veil-thin black cloth over the windows, turning the ambient light ashen.

I could feel the despondency of those children, of these adults. It swirled about the room, now, its rawness overwhelming, and within it I experienced the first inkling of appreciation I had ever had of the fact that my father had lived most of his life without a father of his own. And then it became too much for me.

"Do you remember what the weather was like that day?" I said, asking the blandest question I could think of.

"No," said Eve, practically sputtering, chopping one hand into another. "The date, yes, April 9, 1943, but I don't remember anything about the weather. We were not told anything. That was it. Life was normal."

[8]

Two paintings by her brother Pauli brightened the living room. Directly above the couch hung a large canvas of burnt orange and mustard yellow sunflowers crowded into a vase, the brush strokes busy, the flower petals curved and alive. On the opposite wall was a rare diversion from his van Gogh obsession, a painting of the Margaret Island gardens, a Danube landmark. I thought of Pauli's strict commitment to replication and wondered whether the source had been a photograph or a postcard. I recalled the way my grandmother spoke of him, with the special radiance she shined on the men she loved most. And then in the painting I noticed an older woman in a yellow suit seated on a park bench in front of the lily pond. The suit shimmered against the dark greens and browns of the forest gardens behind. I looked more closely. He had added her to the scene.

I removed the paintings from the wall. "Are these on the list?" I asked my father. He shook his head and jotted them down as I began to wrap them in old blankets.

My father was looking worse as the morning wore on. He had been a handsome man in his youth, old photos documented that, so one could imagine how my mother had been attracted to the dark-haired immigrant with green eyes, plump lips, exotic accent, and gentle manner. In pictures of our young family, there was an easy self-assurance in his stance, ambition and promise on his face. In his thirties and forties, he held a series of prestigious positions, legislative aide to a US senator, presidential appointee in the State Department, senior economic advisor in a major development bank. I remembered occasional Saturday visits to his Capitol Hill office as a young boy, the suite dark and quiet, my father showing me the various call buttons on the side of the senator's desk, the smoky scent of leather that welcomed me as I sat in the senator's chair. As he accumulated accomplishments, the sedentary nature of these roles caused him to put on weight. Worried about his health, or maybe because she wanted to preserve the mother's ideal of her boy even as she reveled in his success, my grandmother alternately scolded and pleaded with my father about his growing midsection. Once she told him she would pay him fifty dollars for every pound he lost and kept off, one of a string of challenges she had proposed and he had ignored. But this wager he accepted, and in a matter of months he slimmed down. Carefully selecting and weighing his food at every meal and exercising several times a week, he shed twenty pounds. When he half-jokingly asked her to pay up, she laughed, and when he protested in mock outrage, she only laughed harder. Perhaps she did not think it right for a son to collect on a bet with his mother. Perhaps she believed, correctly it turned out, that he could not maintain his achievement. In the months since his mother's collapse, he had put on still more weight, as if to goad her into getting better so she could chide him about it.

In the bottom chest drawer, I found a small photo album. I opened the worn cardboard cover to a black and white snapshot of a young woman seated on a bed, wearing a silk bathrobe, her nightgown just visible at the top of her breastbone. It was my grandmother, probably in her twenties. She looked into the camera, her eyes clear, a slight smile on her lips, seeming both self-conscious and expectant. One hand rested in her lap, and with the other she held a book. In the person that I knew, vitality glowed within a hard and weathered shell, yet there in the young woman, it radiated from the surface. The only way I had known my grandmother was as an old woman. Old was the single image of her in my mind, and I felt disoriented as my way of seeing her now shifted, the word Granny taking on new meaning, encompassing the word Maria.

I turned back to the blank cover, wondering what the album was all about, then I looked around. My father was putting small strips of colored tape on the few pieces of furniture that were not going to be donated. Eve was stuffing old plastic grocery bags into a large trash bag. I tilted the album up in my lap and turned the page to a picture of my grandmother at one of the oars of a two-person sculling boat. Standing in the shallow waters of what must have been the Danube, holding the boat in place, was my grandfather. He wore a white swimming cap and a one-piece, muscle-man bathing suit, and he frowned at something in the distance, his expression serious, authoritative. I thought of the portrait of the young World War I cavalry officer in the study and imagined him leading men into battle. His chin was slightly elevated, and one could see how he may have endured the hardships of a Russian prisoner-of-war camp with a sense of superiority and dry humor. But that had been when he was in his twenties, and his youth and military dress reinforced in me a certain inability to connect with him. He had seemed much more a distant cousin than my grandfather. But, seeing him with my grandmother and his sisters in the apartment photo and standing here in the Danube, I felt close to him, and a sense of what I had missed by never having known him.

There they were on the balcony of their Budapest apartment. My grandmother held a book on her lap, knees together, back straight, a soft smile on her face. My grandfather stood beside her, one hand in the pocket of a three-button suit jacket, his head cocked to one side, his eyes enlivened by a jovial squint. A few pages more, and now the two of them were under a chuppa, surrounded by bearded men in wide-brimmed dark hats and a lone woman. The scenes were somehow clearer than the photographs themselves, and I longed to be with my grandparents, on the balcony, by the chuppa. The moments were being lived at my fingertips, the book grew warm in my hands, and for a moment it disappeared and I had the experience of joining them. I turned the page delicately.

"Goodness," I whispered. My grandmother and grandfather were in what might have been their dining room, surrounded by ornate vases filled with flowers. She wore a dark knee-length dress and leaned into him, her head back. His right arm cradled her head, his left held her waist, his mouth pressed deeply upon hers. The kiss was staged for an unseen photographer, but I sensed something true in the way she relaxed in his arms, in the way he bent into her a bit more than necessary to maintain balance.

The images were so real I could barely look at them, and yet I could not stop. On the last page of the album was a photograph of my grandparents standing side by side in a city park. The foliage and the absence of overcoats suggested summer. They were well dressed, perhaps on their way to a concert or the opera. My grandfather clasped a pair of white gloves with one hand, and with the other he held my grandmother and pulled her into his chest. Her left ankle was bent a little away from him, reflecting shyness. They had honest eyes and soothing expressions. Perhaps there was a small café in the park, and I daydreamed about how pleasant it might have been to visit with them over coffee before the performance.

My father was making his way around piles of clothes toward the back of the room, and as he passed me, I held up the picture. He stopped and regarded his parents for a long time.

"They look content, don't you think?" I said.

My father nodded.

"His sisters never accepted her," said Eve, appearing behind me. "She didn't have much say in anything."

I looked back at the picture.

"I don't think it was a match made in heaven, because their backgrounds were so different," Eve said.

I closed the album and held it tightly between my hands. My father continued on to the back room. I scanned the area around me for something that needed doing.

"My mother's family was poorer, from the countryside, very Jewish, not like the Szabos. My father's family was urban, well-off, and they had all converted."

Again, I sought a task to which to excuse myself, and as I did so, I thought about a phone conversation I had had with my grandmother in between our meetings in the city. Around the time of the call, someone had asked me whether I was related to a Szabo they knew in Chicago. As I explained that we did not have any other Szabo family here, it had occurred to me that this question came up quite a bit, given how obscure the name had always seemed. This lingered with me, and a few days later, I found myself thinking about the fact that most of the time the people posing the question were not Jewish. When I asked my grandmother why we seemed to be the only Jewish Szabos I knew of, she told me it was a very common Hungarian name. "Like Smith," she said.

There was a long pause, which she broke by saying, "Many years before the war, people, they converted. And some of these people, and some people that did not convert, they changed their last names, took Hungarian names. There was so much loyalty to Hungary, in the city especially."

I thought of my grandfather, stiff and yet at home in his military uniform, and of his transfer from the factory on Czechoslovakia so his children could be born in Hungary. And still I struggled to understand a sense of nationalism so strong it would motivate one to change one's name.

"So did you change your name?" I asked.

"*Nem,*" she said, "no, dear."

I recalled the repeated response I gave to others, "No, we don't have any other Szabo family here," and the vague sense of incompleteness. Her answer disappointed me.

"Sándor did. Well, his father, he did," she said.

"What did they change the name from? Do you know?" I said, feeling lifted.

She paused. "Gansel," she said, and she spelled it for me.

As I thought about that call, I understood the distinction Eve was trying to make, between city and country, those who had changed their names and those who had not. It was difficult to imagine my grandmother as a timid country girl. To me, she was as urban as can be, and she never shied from speaking her mind. But there was a softness in her pictures in the old photo album, and an authority in Alexander's bearing and the way he held her.

"She never saw herself as strong," Eve said, pressing the point. "Everything was terrible and stressful for her, she was always hysterical." She spoke rapidly. "She would lose things. She suspected the cleaning girl, thought she was stealing. So she always locked everything up." Eve smiled, as if becoming aware of her accusing tone, but she did not relent. "After my mother's mother would visit us, my father would to put on a babushka, pretend to pick up the satchels, and impersonate her. How we would laugh!"

"That's funny," I said, placing both hands on the cover of the album. "When she talked about him, she always glowed."

"I'm glad you said that," she said. "See, like I said before, she had a father who was abusive, so that set her up to worship somebody who was kind, right? I think that's why she adored him. And my father was good-looking, tall, intelligent." She paused, her palms turned up, chin thrust out, as if the case was closed. Then she dropped her arms and added, "I believe when I was born I did the worst thing to her."

"Competing?"

"I didn't. I was just born," she said, whining like a young teenager. "He worshiped me. When I was a baby, on the maid's day off, my mother didn't want to do the housework, especially the diapers. My father said, 'I'll do them. That's pure gold!' and he washed them and boiled them." She stopped, triumph in her eyes. "I took away the love of her life. I think that explains a little why we fought so much later on. She was insecure, and when she saw how much he loved me, she got scared and hurt. But then when Dani was born, she had a man again."

She looked at the empty hallway, to the back room where my father was noisily stacking books as he removed them from the bookshelf.

"That stayed with us all our lives." Her tone offered hints of empathy, then it chilled. "When he died, there was this huge void. The way my mother thought of my father," she said, squinting at me, "that's the way I thought of my father. A god." She shook her head. "My only contact with affection was my father."

The palpable pressure of her gaze lessened, the wrinkles around her eyes smoothed, and her eyes grew shiny, though still dark. I felt a sense of loss in myself, too. My father passed by us and went into the kitchen. Anger rose from somewhere. Why was she telling me all this? I asked myself testily. Why did she attack their relationship, see only imbalance and insecurity? Why did she seem so obsessed with my grandmother's attitudes toward men? I realized I had been holding my breath, and as I exhaled, I saw broader outlines to my resentment. I adored my grandmother. I drew joy and strength from the belief that my grandmother and grandfather had been passionate and true to one another. Eve's comments were not only an attack on my grandmother, but a threat to this piece of my identity. I hesitated, words fell back down my throat, and then I heard my father call from the kitchen.

"Dishes, Peter, do you want dishes?"

I tried to refocus on the room around me. "You mean pots and pans?" I answered.

"Yes."

"No, thanks," I said. My grandmother was a great woman, I told myself, still angry. But this failed to comfort me. In the next moment, I was overcome by a desire to possess something of my grandmother's. Then I worried about what others might want, what Eve might want. Raw assertion weakened, but did not fade. I scanned the room, sorting through items in my mind. My eyes settled on a pair of armchairs nearby. The chairs were in good shape, old-looking but not antiques, so Eve's antiques dealer friend could not have been interested. They did not have a great deal of meaning for me, but I guessed they would not for Eve either. The chairs seemed reasonable. But maybe just one, to be safe, I told myself.

"Could I have this chair?" I said to my father and Eve, as my father emerged from the kitchen. There was a brief silence.

"Yes," said my father, looking puzzled.

"Yes," said Eve.

"Thanks," I said, patting the back of the chair.

I looked around again. The closet doors were open, the closets disheveled. The dining table was covered with china and other items to be divided up. Boxes and overstuffed bags of clothes cluttered the living room floor. The place was beginning to come apart.

[9]

Maybe once a season, we saw each other in the city. We lunched and then went to a movie, a museum, or the Met. Though the time commitment was not small, it became less and less burdensome. Initially, I rarely thought of her between visits. Then, I began to call her just to see how she was doing. I congratulated myself on my good deed, done now mostly without my father's prodding. She was polite, even warm, when I phoned, but also always in a kind of vague hurry. While her gratitude seemed real, the chats were brief. One exception was the time I told her about my promotion to deputy commissioner. Then her joy seemed deeper and her interest in the details more sustained. But this was unusual, and when I called a year or so later to let her know I was leaving my job and moving into the city, rather than burrow into my story, we made a plan for a visit, and then she bade me a joyful, and quick, farewell.

[10]

It was well past noon. Hungry and in need of a break, I offered to go pick up lunch for the three of us. I walked up to 108th Street, a wide avenue with a hodgepodge of shops — Russian, Middle Eastern, and Indian specialty stores, a diner, a hairdresser, a dingy grocery store. Instinctively I looked for Cakeland and recalled the large green, neon-script sign that had crowned the storefront. We used to drive past it on the way to her apartment, but we never went inside. It was as if Cakeland belonged to our Maryland lives, existing as the distant place from which Hungarian cakes and cookies came, and to have gone there would have been a rude intrusion. In hindsight, the fact that we did not stop there struck me as related somehow to the short visits to her apartment. Though the bakery had been closed for twenty years, I scanned the roofline around the nail salon and the liquor store for a trace of the old sign and sniffed the air for the dry scent of European cookies.

In the small grocery store, the deli man and the cashier chattered on in Russian as I stood by the deli counter. Eventually, the cashier laughed, shook his head, and made his way to the front of the store, and the deli man turned to me. After several exchanges, he understood my request for two tuna sandwiches on hard rolls and egg salad on a bagel, and I paid the cashier and left. In a nearby smoke shop, I collected chips and soda, then I headed back. As I passed the scruffy yards on the block, I thought of my grandmother's garden. It was small, no more than twenty feet by twenty feet, but it had a simple elegance, green grass ringed by red roses. She tended her roses with a martial regimen of fertilizers and sprays, and the finicky plants responded like eager recruits. While most of the other yards on the block had gone to dirt, her yard was a delight. One time we arrived while she was hard at work, well-dressed except for worn shoes, an apron, and dirty canvas gloves. She had been mulching the soil and pruning the rosebushes back to twelve-inch stumps, preparing the roses for later in the spring when new growth would sprout and bloom. She stood up as she saw us, holding clippers in one hand, thorny clippings in the other. Seven- or eight-years old at the time, I ran up and grabbed the watering can, and she helped me pour a gentle spray on one of the plants.

I reached her building and stopped in front of the now-barren yard. Years ago, new owners of the apartment complex ordered her to remove the roses, offering no explanation. This mindless dictate, resembling in miniature the authoritarian system from which she had escaped, must have stimulated her most powerful fighting instincts. If it had been a test of wills, doubtless she would have worn them down over time. But it was not a test of wills, it was a test of power. And when she was forced to choose between the owners taking out the plants and doing it herself, she chose the latter. I imagined her on that day as she lifted the last rosebush out of the ground, carefully wrapped the root-ball in burlap, then returned to her knees. She pushed soil back into the hole and smoothed the ground with rhythmic circles of her hands. She clapped the dirt off her gloves, her face as empty as the featureless ground. Then she gathered her tools and headed inside. She had spent a quarter century cultivating her lovely garden. What did she feel in those final moments? Was there no shock, no hurt? No, I told myself in the next breath, she bore it like the other losses in her life, subsuming pain to persistence, complaint to silence. And then she put it behind her.

[11]

"Come, dear Peter," my grandmother said, giving my arm a tug, "the Impressionists are this way." The Metropolitan Museum was a labyrinth, but she never lost her way, the routes worn into her memory through decades of repetition. In the Impressionist rooms, she stood for a long time in front of each canvas, bowing to study a favorite technique or a newly discovered nuance. She frowned with the concentration of a young student, and yet her faint smile echoed the contentment of a lay expert who had seen these works hundreds of times. "So beautiful," she said, as if to the artist.

After an hour or so, I checked my watch. My legs were sore, my stomach was empty. I shifted my weight from foot to foot. "Granny," I said, trying to get her attention. I felt a headache coming on.

"Here dear," she said, "the Renoirs, come."

I followed her while deciding what to do next. She examined a painting, and as she did so, her gold earring, then the bit of red on the tip of her nose caught my eye. I studied her face, the smooth pink-and-white cheeks, the spray of wrinkles spreading from her gray eyes nearly to her small ears. She seemed suddenly physically close and immediate—in my life, no longer outside it. How untrue this had been in my youth, I thought. Back then, there had been vacations with cousins, holidays with grandparents, Bar Mitzvahs, anniversaries, family dinners. But these had been with my mother's relatives. My father's family was small and silent in comparison. While interactions with my mother's side were characterized by tumult and joy, there was quiet and an undercurrent of absence surrounding my father's. The story fragments my grandmother had begun to tell me during our visits made the sense of absence more apparent, less subconscious. Experiencing it more tangibly caused me to want to go to that absence. I wanted not simply to hear the stories but to possess them.

It was clear where to start, the escape from Communism in 1949, the only complete story I knew from their life in Hungary. I had heard it before from my father, but he offered what seemed like a well-scrubbed abridgment. I thought that from my grandmother I might learn more, I might feel more. So the next time I phoned her to make a plan to get together, I asked her if she would tell me the escape story over lunch and, hesitating, also asked whether she would mind my tape-recording it. The line went silent for a bit — perhaps she had been making sure she had understood me, perhaps she had reservations. Then she consented.

But now she was looking at paintings, room after room of them, and the afternoon was slipping away. Hunger amplified my frustration and anxiety.

"Granny," I said, my voice loud and insistent.

She stopped, looking as if I had awoken her.

"What about lunch?" I said, embarrassed, but pleased to get her attention.

"You are tired, dear?" she said.

"Not so tired," I said, lying. "A little hungry."

"Yes, yes," she said, her eyes now narrow. "The cafeteria is no good today, too crowded. I was thinking that maybe we would try the Moca."

We walked east toward Second Avenue. Long ago, the area had been a thriving Hungarian neighborhood, but in the 1970s and 1980s, a slew of indistinct high-rise apartment buildings had gone up, old row houses were refurbished, and brigades of young bankers and lawyers had moved in. Now, only a moribund Hungarian church, a thinly staffed Hungarian library, and a single Hungarian restaurant, Moca, remained. As we entered the restaurant, the smell of chicken paprika thrilled my nose. I drew in a deep breath, and for a moment I was a child watching my father and grandmother prepare the dish. He chopped onions and dumped them into a large pot. After a few minutes, she passed him a bowl of raw chicken parts, which he seared, sprinkled with paprika, and covered. While the chicken simmered, my father made *nokedli*, the small, erratically shaped dumplings served with the dish. He spooned a fat lump of dough onto a wooden cutting board, then holding the board over a pot of boiling water, he sliced and slid little irregular logs of the sticky dough into the water with quick mechanical scrapes of the back of a large knife. My grandmother stood next to him and admired his work. She spoke in Hungarian, he answered in English.

I sat on my knees on one of the kitchen chairs and listened. I could not make any sense of Hungarian, but the sound of it, atonal yet strangely rhythmic, entranced me. It had an odd lilt to it, and I imagined an Irishman producing the sound by applying his brogue to gibberish. I was curious why my father responded in English. He understood the language, so why didn't he speak it? Out of regard for me, so I did not feel excluded? Her comments were animated, he was polite, respectful as a young boy might have been. The first bite-size *nokedli* floated up from the bottom of the pot, and as he skimmed it out with a slotted spoon, it struck me that the shape of the *nokedli* was exactly what it had been when it hit the water — after the brief dive from the cutting board, it was scalded, fixed in time.

My mother came into the kitchen. "How is it going, Mother?" she said to my grandmother. "Is everything in order?"

My grandmother chuckled. "Yes, Cor, dear."

"Did Dani tell you about the dinner at the White House?"

My grandmother's eyes widened. "The White House?"

"Yes," my mother responded. "A state dinner for the president of Brazil."

"*Jaj*, that is fantastic!" my grandmother said, staring in awe at my father.

"Oh, yes," he said, not looking up from the pot of dumplings. "They pulled out all the stops for him — fancy china, music. We had to get all dressed up."

He was never one to brag, and he offered up the details reluctantly, yet clearly pleased, like a shy child a little embarrassed by a stellar report card. Her approving glow brought a smile to his face.

"Was the president there?" she asked in a near whisper.

"Mm hmm," he responded, nodding. "We shook hands."

"He is a good man," she said with an earnest frown.

"Yes," my father responded, his face blank. "There were a bunch of protesters outside."

"Communists," she spat. "If it weren't for President Nixon, Communists would be in charge here, too. Terrible."

"Well, I don't know about that," said my father, as he fished out the last of the *nokedli*.

"They are breaking into stores, Danicom, and taking drugs, and dressing like bums, the young people."

"Yes, but...."

"And all the protests, these people, what is it that they want? They are mostly Communists. It's true, I read it in the newspaper."

"You mean you read it in the *New York Post*," said my father, in a teasing tone.

"Yes, I read it in the newspaper," she repeated emphatically, missing his sarcasm.

He lifted the top off the chicken pot, releasing a cloud of vapor and a rich tomato-peppery aroma, and gestured for her to come test it. She closed her eyes, leaned her face into the steam and inhaled. Then she shook in a bit more paprika. When the chicken was done, my grandmother removed it from the pot and examined the red-brown fatty liquid that remained. As she stirred the liquid, small bits of onion and chicken twirled about. She dropped in several tablespoons of sour cream, made a brisk figure eight with a wooden spoon, then added more sour cream and turned the heat up. The gravy bubbled to life. She scooped up a taste and slurped. "Ah," she said with a nod, then, "Ya," and we all smiled.

Waiting with my grandmother in the Moca entrance, I thought about my father. He had given us something in response to those childhood questions about Hungary. He had given us chicken paprika. He cooked it, we shared in it, I had seconds, and often thirds. For years the rich dish proved a satisfactory substitute for memories.

"Two?" said the waitress, a fleshy woman in a puffy, folk-embroidered blouse and a long red skirt. As we sat down, I snatched up my menu and scanned the strange offerings.

Our waiter was a tall, middle-aged man with disheveled hair, bored gray eyes, and thick hands that engulfed his pad and pen. My grandmother chose the stuffed peppers. I ordered the chicken paprika special and pulled out my tape recorder. The waiter looked at the device, then at me, and disappeared toward the back.

"It is on?" my grandmother asked.

"Not yet." I pushed the buttons clumsily. "Okay, there," I said, with a dramatic exhale.

She smiled.

"The escape. Tell me what you remember." I was relieved to see that she did not mind my brusqueness.

"After the war I opened a retail store in the center of Budapest, a lovely place," she began. "Downstairs I sold all kinds of beautiful fabrics, upstairs I made dresses for customers. It was called Nivo, that means 'something fine.' It was on the Vaci utca, in Pest, that is a street open just to pedestrians right in the downtown. Buildings were still being reconstructed from the war. Many stores were opening there, some of them old stores, some new. I had lots of customers. It was hard work, but it was mine." She shrugged and swept her bangs to the side.

"One day when I came home from the store, my mother said that some men had been to the house to get me to join the Communist Party. Communist?" she said, her lips puckered as she rocked back and forth. "*Nem*. I was no Communist. Hungary was a democracy. We worked for what we had.

"This was 1949, the Communists were getting stronger because they had the Russians behind them. They had a list, a blacklist. People told me that if I was on the blacklist I could lose the store, even go to prison," she said, her eyes big and round. "It was true. Some people had been taken away. But I could never join. Impossible. When they came back on Saturday, I told them I am not joining because I am already a member of the Socialist Party. It was a lie." Her dismissive look suggested nothing could have been more ridiculous than her being a socialist. "I knew I was going to be on the blacklist."

The waiter brought our soups, and I drank mine down. My grandmother's grew cold as she spoke.

"I had a very good friend who helped make arrangements to get us to Vienna. Austria and Hungary, they had been an empire," she said, spreading out the word as she held her arms wide. "Now the border between them was closed, fortified by the Communists. This friend had connections to a man who lived near the Czech border, which was less guarded than Austria." She pointed up in the air. "We went that way instead.

"We left everything but what we could carry. We took a train northeast to Sátoraljaúhely, and walked along the highway. It got dark, then a car came and we got in. The driver left us near the border. We met another man there and some people hiding in the woods, old people, young people with babies, then we started walking. We walked all night."

I imagined the group, silent and anxious. The dark figures wore long coats and carried small sacks.

"We did not speak to each other. I remember that we walked on the leftover stalks in the cornfields. In Hungary, friends told me that we should escape before the harvest, because the corn would hide us while we were walking. But the week before we were supposed to leave, Dani broke his leg showing off on his bicycle, so we had to wait. By the time we left, the fields had been cleared." She laughed. "We crossed into Czechoslovakia, and they took us up to the top of a barn to hide. Somewhere during the walk, or in the barn maybe, I lost my wallet. Other people had money and during the day they hired cars with drivers. We had to find someone who would take us on credit. There was a very nice driver, I will never forget him. He took us through the Tatra Mountains, a beautiful area that was once part of Hungary."

"He drove you across Czechoslovakia?" I said, reaching across the table and touching her hand.

"Yes, yes," she said. "It was a sunny day and the children were so happy. He drove us to Pozsony, or Bratislava, as the Czechs now call it. Emery's relative lived in Bratislava. That is not far from Vienna."

Emery was her second husband. I had not known he had had a hand in any of this. "Emery? How was he involved?"

"I am sorry, dear." She bowed apologetically. "He left Hungary for America in 1938. I knew him since we were children. I married him. He came back for the wedding. Maybe it was July. Anyway, this relative, he was afraid the police would think he was hiding people. So, when he heard we had arrived, he went to his bedroom and pretended that he was sick! He did not even come out to greet us." She trilled the r in "greet" hard and shook her head.

"We were supposed to stay there overnight and get a little rest, but *nem*," she said. "The wife, she would not let us stay. We had to leave in one hour. One hour," she said, leaning in and tapping the table with both index fingers. "She paid off the driver and gave us something to eat. Then a guide came to the apartment. We took a trolley with him until we got to the end of the line, a village called Ligetujfalu, near the border. That is the Czech-Austrian border."

"A little town, you must have stood out," I said, sipping a cup of tea I did not recall having asked for. "A mother and two children, suitcases."

"No suitcases. But, yes, everyone was watching us. At one time there was a man on a motorcycle who came toward us." She looked down the aisle between the tables as if looking down the village street. "I was sure this was a policeman, but he turned around and drove away. Anyway, the guide was going to hide us in his house until morning. He left us in some tall grass to go and check the house. When he came back, he said his wife told him the police had been there. It was not safe. We had to keep going, to walk another night. That is when we crossed the Czech-Austrian border. At one point your father was so tired he threw himself on the ground and said he could not walk any farther." She thumped her hands on the tabletop. "The guide said to him that if he was a soldier he would have to walk until he died. He got Dani up and Dani kept walking."

She chuckled, shook her head, then grew serious.

"Very early morning we arrived at some kind of wooded area where there was a highway that went to Vienna. The guide went for a car and told us to lie down in a ditch near the highway and wait. A peasant was working in a field close by. Many trucks with Russian soldiers drove past, and I was afraid that they were going to see us. Millions of mosquitoes came and we were bitten all over." She wiggled her fingers in the air and tapped her cheeks. "I never forget that. It was terrible." She paused, and the eyes that met mine were shiny. "We were all very upset. Dani and Eve, they were crying, complaining. They wanted to go back home. I was sorry that I took my children out to nowhere."

She broke a piece of bread, sopped up the last of her gravy, and stuffed the bread into her mouth. She nodded as she chewed and gazed at the people around us, white-haired émigrés—women in neat polyester outfits, men with loose-fitting suits, white shirts, and awkwardly knotted ties. Where had they stood when neighbor informed upon neighbor, when livelihoods were taken as the Communists took over? Where had they been when my grandmother escaped? Under the Communists, they might well have been border guards. They might have been Nazi collaborators. It occurred to me that they even might have been both.

"You waited a long time?" I said.

She looked at me and nodded.

"Hours. All night. Early in the morning a car arrived and stopped at the place where we were hiding. We got in the car, and the driver took us through the Vienna checkpoint to the Rothschild Hospital. Emery met us there. The driver asked for a hundred dollars, and Emery made a big scene, didn't want to pay. Finally, he paid," she said, mild disgust escaping from her pursed lips.

The waiter cleared the table, looking us over as he did so. Then he returned with two plates of limp walnut palacsinta.

"You married Emery to get out," I said, half asking, half stating.

She did not flinch. "I would have married the devil," she said as she rapped her knuckles hard on the tabletop. "Anybody would have, to get out of Hungary. I could not live under Communism."

"Was Emery so much better?" I said impulsively.

She stared at me, her expression telling me how much I would never understand about those times, her decisions.

"Check?" said the waiter as he rushed by.

"Ah, food!" my father shouted as I returned with the sandwiches.

We sat in the living room and ate without speaking.

"Peter dear, if you would like the other chair, you can have it," Eve said to me after a while. "Why not have the pair?"

I nodded.

"Is there an extra sandwich?" my father asked, having finished well before us.

I shook my head and handed him my bag of chips.

After lunch, I searched through the papers on my grandmother's old writing desk. I came across her checkbook and skimmed the register. A line caught my eye: August 9, American Sweepstakes, $8. I turned to the previous page and saw entries for small amounts to Reader's Digest Sweepstakes, Publishers Clearinghouse, and again to American Sweepstakes. Similar payments crowded most of the pages. I guessed that when she reached a certain age, the sweepstakes companies, maybe just one or two of them at first, started to send her regular mailings. *But why take the bait?* a voice whined in my head. She had always seemed so self-assured in her judgments of other people's motives, I thought, trying to steady myself. What had overwhelmed her powerful skepticism? Possibly the repeated solicitations wore her down, conditioned her to respond. After the first check, her name undoubtedly was sold by one company to others, and what started as a trickle of prospecting became a ferocious deluge. But why did she continue? She was a romantic and perhaps she fantasized what she would do with her winnings, I guessed. She did not seem greedy, but maybe there was a wish for more comfort, not only for herself, but for her family, too.

I fingered the register. There was something haunting in the number, the frequency of the small checks. She was old. Time was running out. Perhaps that was it. I flipped through the entries again and grew nauseous. Maybe she had been losing control of herself. I called my father over and showed him the checkbook.

"Sweepstakes?" he said as he thumbed through the pages. "Eve told me she and Ed had had a talk with her, told her they were a sham, practically yelled at her." He shook his head. "I guess there was no way to stop her."

I returned to the chest of drawers, and from a drawer I pulled out the photo albums of trips, coworkers, and friends, all unfamiliar. I held one of the albums in my hands, uncertain about whether to save or discard it. I looked up, hoping for help, but Eve was in the back and my father was in the dining room closet. I worried that I might make the wrong decision, get rid of something that was important to my grandmother. Reaching for a reason to shirk the job, I told myself only she could say for sure, and I turned to put the album aside for her to judge. I hesitated, set the album in my lap, and stared at the wall for a minute. I opened the album, leafing through the pages as I might a magazine in a dentist's office, then I threw it into the trash.

My father removed more pictures from the walls and put them on the sofa. Eve shuttled back and forth from the hall closet to the dining room with armfuls of clothes. She tossed most of the outfits into an area in the middle of the room we had designated for donations, a few she set in a box she was taking with her. I took a bunch of letters from a drawer and began to sift through them. Every now and then I came across one I had written her—my Bar Mitzvah thank-you note, a card from summer camp, correspondence from college and travels. They stood out like mile markers on a dark highway. A long dispatch from France included an analysis of the country's political situation and a rhapsodic description of a mountain hike. The information was familiar, but the light of the writer's passion seemed too bright to have been my own.

I put my letters aside and began to dispose of the rest of the drawer's contents. Playing cards, trash. Vacation souvenirs, more trash. Next to these was the faded plastic bag of old documents I had discovered earlier. I slowed, slid the documents out, unfolded the top one, and tried without success to make sense of it. My father was sorting cloth napkins at the dining table. "What's this? *Allampolgarsagi bizonyitvany*," I said, stumbling over the words.

"I don't know, ask Eve," he said, not looking up. "Her Hungarian is much better than mine."

I held the paper in front of Eve as she made her way to the living room with another bundle of clothes.

"Proof of citizenship certificate for Apu, for my father. August 30, 1941."

I looked down at the paper, then at her. "What would he have needed that for?"

"I don't know," she said, dumping the whole load on the hip-high giveaway pile and disappearing into the back hallway.

There was very little text on the faded, unevenly inked certificate. I ran my fingers over the page, trying to divine its meaning from the faint texture of the typewritten letters. My grandfather had taken an action and the action produced a document, which I now held. As I stared at the paper, unable to penetrate its silence, the artifact went cold in my hands.

I picked up another. "*Testimonium de baptism*," I said out loud, hoping to catch their attention. "A baptism certificate? For whom?"

My father leaned over my shoulder. "'Irma,'" he said, repeating the name on the sheet. "That's Eve."

"Baptism?" I said to my aunt as she appeared and bent over the document.

"'Born: Budapest, 1930, March 31. Baptized: 1939, December 14,'" she read. "'Address: Bulyovszky utca 27. Sixth District.' That was our apartment," she said, smiling. "'Document issued: 1944, September 28.'" She straightened as she finished. "I studied the Catechism. I was maybe nine or ten. We all converted. I presume they thought, like many other people did, that we would escape the horrors, which we were not told about. We lived in a children's world." She headed back to the hall.

When the subject of conversion had come up earlier, in the context of the photograph of my grandmother and grandfather, the aunts, and the two husbands, I had felt relieved that there had been no mention of my father in this regard. Now I shuffled through the papers, wary of what I might find. Eve had been converted: The document established that fact. And if she had, why wouldn't my father also have been? I reached the bottom of the pile without encountering a second certificate. This eased my anxiety enough for another question to arise about Eve's document. She had been converted in 1939, but the document was dated September 1944. The Allies had landed in Normandy months before. The war would soon be over. Why obtain a copy of a conversion certificate then? I thought of the books I had purchased on World War II and the Holocaust in Hungary but never read. Hungary always had felt so distant. But in reflecting on the flash of desire that had spurred me to buy the books, and the subsequent numbing of that desire that kept the books on the shelf, I began to understand that it had been made to feel distant, that bringing it closer would take a substantial measure of conscious resolve. Not just now, though, I told myself, scanning the half-dismantled apartment. I paused, then put the documents in a box of things my father was going to take home.

My father returned from carrying a bag out to the trash cans and sat down on the slice of the sofa that was not covered with stacks of pictures. He was quiet for a time, and I forgot he was there.

"After my father died," he said, "my aunts did not like it that I did not have a man in the house. I was ten. They decided to send me to Jesuit boarding school in the south. It was several hours by train from Budapest." He looked as if he was wrestling with a tangle of vines in his memory, then he nodded. "Kalocsa was the town. Boys my age up through high school." He paused. "I remember we wore a military uniform. The hat was yellow with a white brim—the colors of the papal flag."

I imagined him deboarding the train — had he traveled alone? — greeted by an expressionless man in brown robes.

"I had that hat for a long time," he said with a smirk that was part irony, part pride. "I was there from the fall after my father died in 1943 until school was suspended the following spring.

"We had chapel in the morning, then breakfast. Then we went to school. After lunch, there was studying the whole afternoon. There was some play late in the day, and then to bed. A lot of military drilling in the courtyard." I felt the ache of the hungry ten-year-old sitting in chapel before breakfast, the joy of his evening play.

"Sounds like something a young boy might almost enjoy," I said, encouraging him to tell me more.

"I don't know," he said, wrinkling his nose and staring across the room. "There was no heat in the dormitory. Everybody had a washbowl, and it was so cold you had to break the ice in your bowl to clean up. It was sort of scary."

"Sometime in the spring of 1944, my mother sent my Uncle Pauli down to get me. I remember that going home the train was unusually crowded. On the train Pauli told me I had to wear a yellow star." He looked sad and confused. His hands had been resting on his knees, and now he turned up his palms. "I couldn't understand why." He shook his head. "I mean, I did have a vague notion that my parents were Jewish. When I went to the Jesuit school, I registered with the police in Kalocsa. I remember asking one of the police how to spell Israelite." He chuckled. "So I guess I knew, and they knew." He leaned toward the coffee table and picked up the TV remote control.

"Who knew? The police and the priests?"

"Yes, but basically I knew nothing about Judaism. I thought I was a good Catholic boy," he said. It sounded more like a question than a statement. He turned the remote control in his hands, his expression resembling that of a truant child in a school principal's office.

Even so, I sensed he wanted to say more. "What was the star like? Was it pinned to your clothes?" I asked.

"It was fabric. 'Sewn to all your clothes on the left side,'" he said, as if reading a proclamation. "External clothes like jackets. It was yellow, canary yellow." He laughed, though it sounded more like a cough.

I nodded, meditating on his confusion. I saw him in chapel, kneeling on a hard stool, praying to Jesus, imagining him in his mind. One of the priests tapped him on a shoulder, whispered his removal, and a couple of hours later he was on a train, jostled by anxious passengers, a bright yellow Star of David on the chest of his long wool coat. I began to experience confusion myself, and I thought about the difficulty I had attaching myself to Judaism.

"But that didn't last long," he said quickly. "We went underground with papers, thanks to my mother." He looked down and was quiet for a minute. "That was when we moved from Bulyovszky utca to Arany János 29, a building my uncle's family owned."

Eve shouted from the hallway. "It was to collect them easier."

I did not know what she meant at first. Then I realized. She was talking about their move.

"They put them in Jewish houses," she said. "My aunt had this beautiful, huge apartment. Jews could only have one room, so the apartment was divided and that's where we all lived, five or six of us. The whole building was filled with Jews."

I did not stop looking at my father. "You thought you were Catholic, then you were Jewish, I mean...." The question collapsed. What I wanted to know in that moment seemed simple. I regrouped. "How did you feel?"

He put the remote back on the coffee table. "I have no idea," he said, sounding helpless. "Nobody asked how we felt."

Suddenly I was angry. "But I'm asking you now."

Eve entered just then. "This is my mother's heroism," she said, wagging a finger at me. "The apartment building had these huge doors, and we were locked in every night until nine in the morning. But at five a.m. the super let her out to get on line at the Swiss embassy for protective papers. She went out without a star, risked her life."

My father straightened and his gloom seemed to have passed. "But before that, there was bombing, much more than before," he said eagerly. "We went to sleep still dressed. When we heard the siren, we had two minutes to get to the cellar." He smiled. "The building superintendent and his wife, they were a nice couple. Jews could not have radios, but they had one, and we used to listen to the news at seven or eight o'clock. 'This is the BBC calling Hungary,'" he said in an announcer's tone, urgency in his voice. "And then there would be these musical tones, 'Da, da, da, doon. This is the BBC calling Hungary.'"

Then the glow in his eyes disappeared.

"Late at night the Nazis would come," he said. "Usually two o'clock in the morning. Bang on the external door of the building, 'Everybody down!' We would go down to the courtyard, and they would check papers. It was different in Europe than here. Everyone had papers there, a document that said who they were, where and when they were born, where they lived, their occupation, their religion, stuff like that. They always took away one or two men who didn't come back."

I pictured rumpled and sleepy families milling in the courtyard, doing their best to stand in a straight line. A wave of tension stiffened the group as an officer in shiny boots examined their papers, flanked by several soldiers. The officer flicked his head at a middle-aged man and the soldiers grabbed him as his wife's shoulders shook under her overcoat. At least his father had not gone like this, I thought for a moment, and then I blinked away the vision.

"What else did they say when you were in the courtyard?"

"I don't know," he said. "We were all terrified, that's all I remember, scared shitless." He looked away, embarrassed at having felt fear in a frightening situation. I wanted to comfort him and started to say something, but Eve chimed in.

"From there we went to another apartment on the Danube where a lot of people with Swiss protective papers went," Eve said. "People were sleeping on the floor it was so crowded. Sometimes the Hungarian Nazis came and took people out of these buildings. They took them to the Danube where they were going to shoot them. And many times they didn't." She shrugged.

"That must have been terrifying," I said.

"Yes, but they never took us," she said. She seemed to be making an argument to me, or to herself, that somehow because they had survived, it had not been awful. "And not everybody was shot."

I wanted to open the memory up, to see it alongside them, to take in every harrowing dimension, to bear some of their burden. "But—"

"We just...." she said, cutting me off. Then she relaxed. "I think I became petrified wood."

"Where was this?" my father asked her, the lines on his forehead deep.

"After Arany János 29, by the Danube," she said forcefully.

"Were we all there? I don't remember." He was challenging her in his own indirect way, even while trying to unearth the memory in his mind.

"Yes, of course," she said. "Then we got Christian papers. You know Faludi Magdi? Granny's good friend in Hungary?"

"No," I said.

"She still writes these wonderful letters from Hungary about politics, about everything. Anyway, her husband got papers for my mother. The papers said she was a school teacher, a spinster living with her mother. So my grandmother got papers, too. Dani had papers from somewhere else, which left me out, but not purposely, of course," she said, holding her chin up.

"One of the ladies in Uncle Miklós's office, she got me the papers," said my father. "I was a refugee from the southern part of Hungary. My parents were killed. I was an orphan." He seemed still to be rehearsing his identity in case his documents were inspected.

"I had no papers," said Eve, ignoring him. "My mother's idea was to go to the parents of my school friend — Eva Schmidt was her name — and ask them if we could use her papers. They could say her papers were lost and get another copy. It was a big city, big enough for two Eva Schmidts." She laughed and clasped her hands in her lap. "They refused. And what did my mother do? She went with two witnesses to the town hall and got papers that said I was Eva Schmidt." She laughed again. "This was my mother."

"Then my mother, grandmother, and Jancsi *néni*, they moved to Üllői út, to another building my uncle's family had."

"Our mother took Eve to a convent," my father said, looking at her. "Maybe she told the nuns a story that Eva Schmidt lost her parents in the air raids. I don't know."

I thought about the copy of the baptism certificate. "That was in the fall of '44?"

He shrugged and continued. "Then she put me in this Nazi-oriented orphanage for boys near the Városliget. I remember putting on a Hungarian Nazi armband without any thought." He patted his bicep.

I chuckled at her audacity — not just an orphanage, but a Nazi-oriented orphanage. Who would be so crazy as to try to hide a Jew there?

"It was like a big game," he said. "I knew about Catholic stuff, and nothing about Judaism, so it was not difficult to make-believe. Plus, I was not circumcised. Sometimes they made people pull down their pants. But not there. That was grown-ups anyway. I was never asked for documents." He sighed and paused. He looked tired, and I thought in passing that the flow of memories must be exhausting him. I turned to Eve.

"What happened to Bözsi and Margaret? They didn't go to Üllői út with you?"

"No," said Eve. "They did not have to. They were converted Catholics for thirty years, so they were considered really converted. Also, there was this connection to Szálasi. They had a mark on their apartment that distinguished them from the rest of us, that helped protect them."

Eve looked at me and nodded, sensing my awareness of how slim, how artificial, had been the lines between safety and peril. Then she rose and returned to the hall closet.

"My mother moved me from the orphanage to another apartment house," my father said.

"You were in someone's apartment?" I said.

"No, I was in a basement. Everybody lived in basements at that time. It was dark and crowded. Very often there were no lights, just candles." He wriggled his fingers. "It was almost winter and starting to get cold. The Russians were close enough that there were artillery barrages and intense air raids all the time. I was sort of scared being there by myself in this group of strangers."

One moment I had been engaged with the story, almost in it, and the next I felt outside it, detached. The memories and the emotions they carried seemed to hit an invisible impermeable surface and, like street runoff from a summer downpour, did not sink in. I could not fathom my father's terror amidst the bombardment. The sudden difficulty with empathy unnerved me, and I tried harder, stared more intensely at him.

"Through all these air raids and artillery exchanges, my mother was constantly on the move. She ran from her mother, to my sister, then to me, bringing us food and checking if we were okay. I was told many times not to call her *Anyuka* in public, because in our papers we were unrelated, but I always did." He smiled. "Mommy!" he said, mimicking a child's relieved cry.

I heard a tumble of shoe boxes. "Oh, shit," Eve said from the closet. My father did not seem to notice.

"One time, she was on her way to me but the air raid was so intense she stopped at a nearby building. She banged and banged on the courtyard door, but no one came, so she kept going and made it to where I was. I told her...." He stopped. He took a deep breath and collected himself. "I told her I couldn't stand it alone anymore." He paused again. He met my eyes and shook his head.

"Her papers said she did not have any children, but she took me back with her to Üllői út. Everybody there was afraid that somebody would tell on us. They could have taken her away. Taken *us* away. But it never happened." He rubbed the back of his neck, then squeezed it. "On our way out of the building I had been hiding in, we saw the building next door, the one she had tried to get into during that air raid. It had been leveled by bombs, completely flattened."

He pressed his lips together.

"She was fearless," he said, his eyes glistening with awe and sadness. "I was scared to death."

I looked out the front window through the half-drawn shades. It was still light out, but late afternoon shadows had spread across the yard and begun to darken the room.

[13]

I moved to New York. I had no job, no apartment. It was midwinter. I crashed at a friend's place at Sixty-Ninth and York for six months while I tried to get my footing. I landed a position with a small consulting firm that figured out ways for large consumer product companies to reduce costs. The hiring manager was a refugee of the Giuliani purges and wanted to help out another former government employee. He talked me up to the firm's founder, and she gave me a three-month trial. I had a bit of firm ground.

An acquaintance heard of an apartment opening up on the West Side, and I moved there in August. The place occupied maybe five hundred square feet on the top floor of a six-story, midblock building on Ninety-Seventh Street, just west of Broadway. It had a small kitchen that opened into a living room, a bathroom with poorly chosen seventies-style tiles and fixtures, and a bedroom. Its selling points were low rent and the nearby express train. After I had been there a while, I grew fond of the southern exposure and how it changed through the seasons. In summer, the sun was high and brightened the living room most of the day. In winter, the low-angled light stretched deep into the apartment; that is, when it was not blocked by the two tall buildings across the way, one a recent monstrosity, the other a prewar gem. Faded letters painted down the side of the latter read Paris Hotel, indicating it had not always been a co-op. My building had not always been apartments either. The long-time resident across the hall, whose partner was dying of AIDS, said that at one point it had been a brothel. Riverside Park was just down the street, and in the fall, when the leaves were down, I went frequently to the promenade on Riverside Drive and found a bench with a good view of the Hudson. There I meditated on the strange yet familiar motions of the gray tidal waters, now ebbing out to the Atlantic, and then flowing inland toward Albany.

The company offered me a permanent position. Norah lived three blocks away, and soon we were dating again.

[14]

Though I was living geographically closer to my grandmother than ever, I saw her only once during the time I was settling in the city. I was too busy, first finding work and a place to live, then consumed by the pace of the new job. Things eased just a bit in October, and we met at MoMA for lunch and an old film about Italian partisans in World War II, which was showing in the theater downstairs.

As we shuffled with the crowd toward the theater exit, I had the sensation of having been in the war in dreams, and the idea of war stayed with me, even after we were out on the street. Without thinking, I turned to my grandmother and asked her, "What were you doing during the war?" It was an offhanded question, but posing it kindled an awareness of how little I knew of her wartime experience. There had been nothing about the war in my youth, no family lore, no story scraps.

She pouted and shrugged as she looked up and down Fifty-Third Street, deciding which way to go. "Yes," she said, tying her scarf as I moved close to her. "There was a zoo in the big city park near where we lived, the Városliget. Behind the park was the Shell Oil refinery. The British used to bomb it. One time they missed and blew up the zoo. Many of the animals escaped. They had to shoot them."

"That's awful," I said.

She looked at me and nodded, slipped her hand around my elbow, and then started west toward Sixth Avenue.

"During World War II people who had been officers during World War I could keep whatever they had, such as a store."

"What do you mean?"

"There were laws," she said, "for Jews."

The way she said it, the way I heard it, the laws were for other people, for Jews, not her. Though I was Jewish, I found it difficult to identify with, to appreciate the fact that she was Jewish and had been so in Budapest during the war. It was as if a physical, solid barrier prevented the assembly of facts into realization.

"After my first husband died, because I was his widow I could keep his store. He had left a debt, big money for back then. I ran the store, paid off the debt. Then the Germans came in. March 19, 1944. I never forget that day."

The sun was still strong, infusing late-summer warmth into the cool air. She had picked up her pace as she talked and we were now walking forcefully up Sixth, her gait the stiff march of someone who had spent a lifetime in cities. She took short steps, but she moved with deceptive speed, and I had to strain to keep up with her.

"The next day they said that all the Jewish stores must be closed, even the stores of World War I officers," she said. "The next day!"

"We had to move to a Jewish building, Arany János utca 29. Dani I hid in an orphanage. Eve went to a convent. Later, when the fighting was bad, I moved with my mother to a building on Ulloi Street. We lived in the basement with everyone else. The Germans and the Russians were fighting building to building. One day a Russian soldier broke into the cellar and we were liberated."

She marched on, and I grew winded. I thought of a visit she had made to my parents in Maryland the previous summer, when, after several hours touring the National Gallery, she decided to go see the White House. She proceeded to walk the mile down Pennsylvania Avenue in the mid-August Washington swelter. She had stamina, but I also noticed a voraciousness in her walk that went beyond simple energy.

"Tell me, dear Peter," she said. "How are you? How is the apartment and your work?"

"Not bad," I said. The film and her memories had opened a connection to the war, and her question triggered an abrupt change in orientation that made me feel confused at first. "The apartment is so-so. Great location though. I've got the 2 and the 3 trains right there. Work is work. A lot of travel. I am away most of the week, every week. But the factories are interesting."

As I spoke, I tried to keep my attention in the past, and I groped for a way to turn the conversation back in that direction. Half-conscious visions of the war appeared as shadows in the back of my mind, yet I experienced a sense of familiarity with war, and feelings of safety and calm. This was odd, and I felt a brief pulse of shame, and then images from childhood briefly overcame me. I was nine or ten and two boys from the house next door and I were building a small basin in their back yard in hopes of starting a frog zoo. Around the basin we stretched a chicken-wire fence. Then we grabbed a couple of buckets and nets and headed to the creek down at the end of our wooded suburban block. The frogs proved elusive, and after a half hour I still had not caught my first. Then I spotted one squatting by the bank. Its marble-like eyeballs poked through the water. I circled around the bank, and crawled on hands and knees to the edge. The eyes were still there — two black bubbles floating on the surface. I sprang. I felt the slimy flesh in my hands and looked down on the wriggling creature with disbelief and excitement. I gave a cry of victory, plopped it into the bucket, and went back for more.

It was late afternoon by the time we got back, arms burning as we carried the bucket across the backyard. We filled the makeshift pond with water, dumped the frogs in, and watched them for a while. Then, exhausted, we went into the boys' house for dinner. I stayed over that night and after dinner we built a fortress of blankets and chairs and talked excitedly of our plans for the pond. We would plant grasses and seaweed. We would catch fish and add those. Eels, too. I fell asleep to the sound of crickets and, I imagined, the croaks of frogs.

In the morning we rose early and rushed out to the pond, still in our pajamas. There we stood, speechless, our fingers gripping the scratchy chicken wire. The frogs were gone, the basin empty. After a minute we all burst out laughing. We laughed until we lost our breath. We laughed until our sides hurt. We laughed at the frogs and their uncertain fate. We laughed at our pond. We laughed at ourselves. We laughed without reason. And then we laughed some more.

Once we had eaten and seen a film, my grandmother usually made for the subway, but she did not mention the R train as we walked briskly past the station entrance. I sensed that she wanted to stretch our time together that afternoon. When we reached Central Park, she stopped, looked around, then turned west toward Columbus Circle.

I caught my breath, then patted her hand, which was still curled over my elbow. "So the Russians took over?"

"Yes," she said. "After the war there was not so much to eat. Dani, he used to beg me for butter." She stopped walking. "No, not butter. Lard," she said, as she started moving again, "for his bread. One time I went to the countryside. I had still some fabric from the store and I exchanged it for food with the peasants. We were in the square of a small town when some Russian soldiers came. Everybody ran because they would take people away for labor in Russia. I had on a pair of overalls and a coat. Every pocket was full, and I had a knapsack, too." She lifted her purse and shook it.

"I tried to climb a fence to get away, but I got stuck. A soldier came, and he poked me with his bayonet. When he saw I was a woman, he laughed and walked away. It was a miracle!" she stopped and chortled. "When I got home, Dani's eyes were so wide! I weighed forty-nine kilograms, and the food I carried in pockets and bags," she said, as she touched her sides and then held out her arms as if they carried the very bags, "weighed fifty kilograms!"

I imagined my father as a boy, slathering the lard on his bread. She was still laughing, and for a moment she had the lively expression of a little girl. It faded in and out as I studied her face, searching for more of it.

"Ice cream?" she said suddenly.

A pushcart had somehow materialized in front of us. The late-fall warmth had brought out the street vendors, keen for a final infusion of cash before winter set in. They had appeared as crocuses do in unusually mild spells during that time of year, bright and eager, yet out of place for the season.

"Why yes," I said. "Chocolate éclair, please."

She paid the man and we started up Central Park West. I extended my elbow for her hand. "Why don't we go into the park?" I said after a bite of the ice cream.

When we reached the park entrance at Sixty-Fifth Street, she hesitated. "It is safe?" she said.

"Oh yes," I said, chuckling.

We turned in and walked along a path in silence, enjoying our treats. War filled my mind again — bombs crashing into the zoo, my grandmother hiding in basements. We sat down on a bench near some ball fields. And then a thought filled an absence in her story. They were Jews. They had hid. I experienced a rush of enlightenment, similar to what a child experiences as they solve a difficult math problem for the first time — the component parts falling into place, the relationship of one to the other understood, the extrapolation of the principle fundamental to so many other things all at once. Holocaust. The word floated into my mind like a thin cloud on a soft breeze, and I searched my memory for a time she or my father had uttered it. No, never. But they had been Jews in Budapest. The Germans had taken over. Never? Sprinting to keep up with my thoughts, a question escaped almost without notice. I looked at my grandmother and said, "How many people you knew were lost in the camps?"

She was quiet for a while. My heart pounded, and a tingling heat surged to my head and my hands.

"About sixty friends and family," she said, staring straight ahead.

"How many were family?"

"Maybe thirty," she said, adding, "They lived in the countryside," in a tone that suggested this explained things.

"Who were they? Can you tell me about any of them?" I asked, filling with anguish.

She did not answer. Her face was pale, her eyes shifting, unfocused.

"My cousins Simon and István, that is, Steven Berger," she said. "With the motorcycle, you remember? He was a decorated officer in the army in World War I."

"Who was?" I said.

"István," she said, her face turning hard and gray. "They didn't care. The Nazis came and they took him away." Her last word, "ah-vay," sounded like a bottle shattering against a wall. "Him and his wife and their children. And his mother, too."

Nearby two teams of children, one in green uniforms, the other in blue, were playing soccer. A boy kicked a ball just past the goalie's outstretched arms and everyone on both teams shrieked.

My mind was on fire. She seemed to say "sixty friends and family" so matter-of-factly. And to have said nothing to me until now? What in her life—

"I have not been to Central Park in nearly thirty years," she said, looking out at the field and the children as play resumed. "Thank you, dear Peter." She tapped me on the thigh and smiled. "I will tell all my girlfriends that I have been to the Central Park." She stood up. "They will never believe it."

[15]

On weekends I took walks in the neighborhood. Before the walk I had brunch at one of the diners nearby. Usually I chose the Metro at One Hundredth Street, sometimes the Strand on Ninety-Sixth, though it grew dingy over time; occasionally it was the Argo, at Ninetieth, where the motto printed on the menu assured the patron that "You Don't Need to Empty Your Wallet to Fill Up Your Stomach." After brunch, I would stroll down Broadway. The length of the walk was a matter of distance and not destination. My legs would start to tire somewhere near Zabar's and I would turn around and head back. Instinct, rather than need, determined stops along the way. I might wander into the antiques shop at Ninety-Third, stop by the bank, poke around Ivy's Books, or browse Harry's Shoes. Fall was my favorite time for Broadway walks, when the low midday sun warmed my face and drew striking shadows around the buildings, the street trees, and the people, making everything so vivid as to heighten the sense of being alive.

Work and travel were so intense that most weeks I entered a kind of stupor, filled with spreadsheets, meetings, and bumpy flights. But from time to time I meditated on what my grandmother had said on the bench in Central

Park, troubled. How little I knew. How little I had been told. How little I had sought to find out. So much was missing. These thoughts rippled at the back of my consciousness. Then on one Sunday walk I found myself at Eighty-Eighth Street pulling open the door to West Side Judaica. The store overflowed with Jewish items. Talises and yarmulkes, Sabbath candles and klezmer CDs were stacked on shelves and stuffed in drawers toward the back. Religious books spread up the wall to the right, from waist to ceiling. In the counter cases in the middle of the store were mezuzahs, candlestick holders, and fancy dreidels. To the left, shelf after shelf was stuffed with books on Jewish history.

"Shalom, good morning!" said one of the several men who worked there in a pleasant voice, though he did not look up. He wore black pants, a white shirt, and a skull cap. *Payot* curled to his shoulders.

I answered and looked around with self-conscious vagueness, as though I were just wandering through, with no particular need in mind. The Judaica, the man and his colleagues, stimulated familiar, complex feelings of inadequacy and distance. For a moment I was back in Hebrew school. It was sixth grade. I was sitting in a school-desk chair in a dark classroom watching a black-and-white documentary on the camps with twenty or so other kids. Walking skeletons, healthy GIs, and bulldozers pushing corpses flickered across the screen. Bodies stacked like sun-bleached stick upon stick in a disorderly mound I forced myself to comprehend as an oversize muskrat lodge. Later, on the basketball court outside the temple library, I received a pass from a friend and made a shot with the worn-smooth ball. We were cutting class again. But we played in plain sight, and I wondered why no one came out and scolded us, half wished for it, as much as I hungered to be out of those rooms. Where were the people who thought it so important to show us the films, but not important enough to shepherd us back inside to learn our prayers?

Beyond the friends, the one thing that anchored me to the temple was the rabbi, Eugene Lipman. He was thickset, with gray-flecked black hair, and black horn-rimmed glasses that framed dark eyes. On holidays his sermons blazed with insights and admonitions. Though he did not smile much, he was not unkind. His intellectual and emotional absorption in Judaism filled all the spaces of his personality such that kindness was at best a faint glow around him. But this did not matter. His intensity thrilled me. He was a serious man, the kind of person to whom it was natural, even comforting, to make solemn promises. Shortly before my Bar Mitzvah, I met with him in his study and he asked me, as he did all of us, to commit to continue through to Confirmation, which meant three more years of Sundays, plus community service. He sat forward in his chair and waited for my answer, his steady gaze welcoming rather than intimidating.

As I watched the men in West Side Judaica chatter away in Yiddish, an anxiousness about the completeness of my attachment to Judaism resurfaced. Not that I had not tried, I told myself, thinking of Seders with friends and services I sought out on high holidays. I felt the hard seat of the balcony pew I had occupied several weeks earlier in the church B'nai Jeshrun used for its overflow service. I looked down at beautiful Hebrew letters in the prayer book, forming the sounds as I followed along with the congregation. It was easier now. Each year I concentrated hard on relearning the Hebrew alphabet, the rhythms, the melodies, until they were mostly recovered. But without fail melancholy overcame me as the service approached the prayer for the dead, the Kaddish. Year after year I studied it, but it never sunk in.

In the Judaica store, I walked over to the wall of history books. The Six Day War, the founding of Israel, biographies were all mixed together, arranged not by author or title, but by an idiosyncratic scheme I could not decipher. I noticed an older woman in a plain skirt and a dark blouse sorting a pile of books by one of the shelves. She wore a wig and unfashionable glasses. Eventually, she looked up.

"Hungary," I said, gesturing toward the texts. "I am wondering whether you might have anything on the Holocaust in Hungary." I sensed a brief break in the conversation behind me, but when I listened for it, the discussion among the men seemed never to have paused. I started to sweat and unzipped my coat and fleece.

"A few," the woman said without inflection, as she walked over to one of the bookcases, running her hand along the uneven row of texts.

"Here," she said, tapping the tops of two volumes maybe ten inches apart. Then she left me and returned to her sorting.

I started to scan the books — something on Christianity and the Hungarian Holocaust, a work about Hungary during the war — then my eyes landed on a faded white book jacket, a little bent and torn at the top. The title on the binding read, *The Hungarian Jewish Catastrophe.* Catastrophe. The choice of words intrigued me. The term was large and dreadful, but also grounded and alive. It was vague, evasive even. What sort of catastrophe? I thought wryly as I pulled the book from the shelf. The only decoration on the faded cover was a fragment of a bright yellow Jewish star. On the title page I found the name of the editor, Randolph Braham, and the phrase under the title, "A Selected and Annotated Bibliography." I flipped through pages filled with hundreds of sources. I will read them all, I vowed with mad determination. Then I sighed. I turned the book over in search of its price. After rent, every extra dollar was going to pay down school debt. Forty dollars, a red sticker told me bluntly. This would not be an inconsequential proportion of what I had left in the bank before the next paycheck. I looked out the storefront window at the people moving past, some flowing, some darting, and followed a flash of yellow from a speeding taxi.

"Anything else?" said the man at the counter, his tone friendly yet impersonal. "Some candles maybe?"

"No. No, thanks," I said, fishing out my credit card. "Just the book."

[16]

"I'm not whining because I think that all this made me strong," Eve said, holding up her empty hands. "He lived there on Üllői út," she said, tilting her head at my father, "and he ate, I suppose, because they lived like Christians. I, on the other hand, was in a convent where they were hiding Jewish children. The Nazis got wind of it and came to take all of us away." She shoved a pile of shoe boxes into a trash bag. "Somebody tipped off the nuns and my mother brought me to Kemeny Oscar, that was my father's best friend and business partner. At that point there was no warning siren, just bombing. Everybody had moved to the cellar, except Kemeny and his wife. Can you imagine, this late in the war?" She did not wait for a response. "One day the building next door was hit by a bomb and the chimney fell and smashed our windows. Finally, they said it was time to go to the basement." She chuckled. "So down we went, and guess who yells to me from the other side of the cellar? A friend from school. 'Hi Irma!' she shouts. Everybody's listening, and I tell her, 'I'm not Irma, I'm Eva, Eva Schmidt.' That was my fake name on the papers my mother got. She didn't understand, kept calling me Irma."

She laughed again.

"Oscar, he was worried, so they hid me in the cellar wood closet. They put a light and a cot in there. Somebody brought me food. I don't know what I did for the bathroom." She paused, seeming to concentrate on something that needed doing in the back room. "I guess I cracked a little in there."

She was fourteen years old. The narrow escapes, the constant risk of death or capture, probably only heightened for her the sense of being without protection, without an anchor, the result of her father's death, her treasured father, some eighteen months earlier. The way she talked about the wood cellar brought into relief how manifold the emotional isolation of her profound loss must have compounded her physical isolation.

"I'm sorry," I said, but she was not listening.

"I didn't see my mother again until we were liberated," she said as she stood up and made for the hallway.

Worn out and hoping to accelerate the day's end, I unplugged a lamp and tied up the cord. My father took a trash bag outside, then he returned and sat on the sofa to rest. He pulled another bag over and spoke as he began to tie it.

"At Üllői út I was befriended by the Germans," he said. "I remember the soldiers walking like there was nothing going on, getting supplies or sitting in trucks, and the shells were falling everywhere. They were impressive, totally unfazed." He looked at the floor and shook his head. "Meat was scarce, and in the courtyard of our building the Germans set up a soup kitchen where they cooked soup for the front line. They cut up horses that got killed by shrapnel and made stew with the meat." He stirred the air with his hand.

I pictured him standing in a corner of the courtyard watching the butchering. Nausea unsettled me, but then a kind of numbness followed, and the scene blurred and my disquiet calmed. The room had grown gray, and I stood and switched on a light. "Did you get any?" I said.

"Get any?"

"Any stew?"

"Oh, I don't know," he said, his face wrinkled in an effort to recall. He exhaled heavily. "Yes, I think I got some stew from them for my family. I was pretty self-assured because I was raised as a Catholic, and so I didn't get nervous asking. It was like a game."

"They put this huge pot in this wagon attached to a horse. A cook and a guard took it to the front, which was maybe two blocks away. Sometimes only one guy came back."

"That must have been weird. Did you know them?"

"I don't remember," he shrugged. "Maybe yes."

He seemed unmoved by this loss of men he had admired, and his distance surprised me. Then I realized I was experiencing the same feeling, or nonfeeling, in that moment, too.

"In a nearby building there was some kind of a hardware store. One day everybody was in there stealing things." He smiled as a child's embarrassment filled his face. "I took a box of pins. When the Russians came there was a big fear. By that time the Germans had no soldiers except kids, sixteen-year-old kids. Somewhere in the basement there was a wounded German soldier. If the Russians thought we had been hiding him, there would have been hell to pay. I remember him moaning a long time. Fortunately, the boy died during the night," he said with visible relief.

"In Budapest the apartment house cellars are connected underground," Eve said, a dustpan and broom in her hands. "The Russians smashed through the walls with tanks to try to get around the Germans." She banged the dustpan against the wall. "There would be a Russian cannon on this corner, and a German cannon on this corner." She pointed at the back room and the bathroom. "And they would shoot at each other. And I remember the megaphones playing the Russian psychological warfare over and over. 'Give up and we will have food and water for you. There is no escape. You cannot win.' Their German was not very good.

"My mother visited me at the Kemenys' and got stuck because our block was liberated while her building was still on the German side. They were the worst criminals, the first Russians. I think they were from the Ukraine." She gestured at me with the broom. "I didn't know you had to be afraid of them because the generals gave them forty-eight hours of free rape." Her tone was hard. "I was in the cellar, and a Russian soldier with an Uzi appeared. The soldier came toward me and everybody shuffled back. But my mother stood in front of me and yelled at him in Czech, which is near Russian. Then she pushed him and he fell over in front of her. He was drunk and he fell right to sleep."

She stood next to me now. "The next day we went back to Üllői út, because my mother was worried about Dani." She shot him a sour look. He was looking at her, but seemed not to hear what she had just said.

"Those soldiers were not the elite, they were the cannon fodder," said my father. "Asiatic, animal-like. I remember seeing this Russian soldier give water to his horse from a mossy wooden pail. First he held up the pail for the horse, then he drank. From the same bucket," he chuckled. "First the horse, then the soldier." He jabbed his finger into his left thigh, then his right. His laughing eyes met mine. "They would come for women to help peel potatoes. 'Peeling potatoes,' everybody knew what that meant." My father glanced at Eve. "But nothing happened.

"My mother got hold of a cart," he said. "We put all our belongings on it and pushed it back to Arany János utca, in the center of Pest. It was a long walk. The buildings we passed were mostly rubble. We saw dead horses, dead people. I watched the bombs coming out of the airplanes."

"They were still fighting?" I asked.

"Yes, but on the other side of the river. The Buda hills," he said. He looked up. "Little metallic tubes in clusters. Drifting west."

"Could you hear them?"

"Oh, yes." He smiled. "Peeeew, bum!" he said, starting high-pitched, then finishing with a low growl as he raised and lowered his head. "Peeeew, bum!"

"Were you afraid?"

"No, no, it was exciting. In any case, after the shock troops, more civilized soldiers came. They only stole watches. I remember one soldier, he opened his jacket and it was lined with watches and clocks. They would say, *Dai mne chasi!* Let's have your watch! I learned that, *Dai mne chasi!* They stole my Aunt Jancsi's watch."

"Hello, dear Peter, it is your Granny." She never left messages on my answering machine. I turned up the volume. "I am sorry but I cannot take the class with you. That is too much money. I do not want to do it."

I heard something strange in her voice, and I sat down, rewound the tape, and listened again. Her usually brassy tone was muffled by a phlegmy cough. But that was not it. Her words sounded rehearsed, and yet she halted as she delivered them. Weakness? I thought. Fear?

Over the winter she told my father she would no longer audit classes at Hunter College, which she had done for two decades. She loved Hunter—the handsome professors, the young students, the knowledge, the wonders each course revealed. But the subway was too much, she had said, and she recounted how on her way to the train after Hunter classes, she had to fight through bursts of passengers exiting up the station stairs, and how on the platform she was jostled about by people crushing onto already stuffed subway cars. When my father related her resolution to me, I felt for her and asked him if there was not something else she could do, something he could find for her. He said he had urged her to look into classes at the senior center near her home in Queens, but she proved deaf to the idea. Queens? For culture? her inaction seemed to say.

Her decision to give up Hunter was the most significant of several recent signs that she had begun to waver, and it disturbed me. I had come to appreciate the calming effect of her life force, the strength I drew from her steady, unflinching character, how her stories illuminated absences within me. In her presence, I understood that my unsettled life resulted from something internal, my own unsettledness, yet I also began to cultivate patience with my chronic ambivalence and acquired a measure of confidence with which to make choices. I worried about her state of mind and what I might lose if her constancy failed.

One Sunday, the 92nd Street Y catalog arrived with the newspaper. Thumbing through it, I came across a lecture series on European cultural history from the Middle Ages to the Renaissance. It met on Saturdays, when there would be no problem with subway crowds. It was the 92nd Street Y, and that had to be sufficiently cultured for her. I called my grandmother. We could take the class together, I suggested. I was making more money and could pay for it. She agreed. All seemed restored.

I played the message again, and before the answering machine had clicked to a stop, I called my father and asked him to plead my case. "I'm trying to do something for her," I said. "The money is not a problem. Please, get her to let me *do* something for her." If my voice had not been shaking, he might have shrugged off the task of trying to convince his mother to change her mind. But a few evenings later the phone rang. It was my grandmother.

In a clear, practiced voice, she thanked me, and told me she would take the class.

In the middle of each lecture there was a half-hour break for bagels and coffee put out by the Y. One sunny April Saturday, we decided to skip the nosh and go for a stroll in the neighborhood. She held my hand as we crossed Lexington and walked slowly toward Park Avenue. We breathed the pleasant spring air and were silent for a time. I wanted to ask about the family, about the Holocaust, but I also felt that, to have any hope of taking this sort of class with her in the future, I needed to be careful to make the experience a pleasant one for her. Yet the weather relaxed me, stimulated a lighthearted reassurance that I could manage things if I went further back in time, to the beginning.

"So tell me about where you grew up," I said, squeezing her hand.

She smiled and, after a minute, she spoke. "My mother and father, they were both from Herend, in the countryside. That is where the famous porcelain is made. My china closet is full of Herendi porcelain, which I bring back from Hungary. The name of the owner of the Herendi factory was Fischer. He and my mother were good friends." She talked at the gentle pace of our walk. "After the war, I am talking about the World War I, my father became a senior advisor in the post office, so we moved to the city, to Buda. We lived at Bercsenyi utca 9, *masodik emelet*. That is the second floor."

She stopped and pointed at me as if instructing.

"*Masodik emelet*. I was just a girl!" she said, laughing in pleasant surprise at finding herself back in a long-forgotten moment. "Anyway, we had a stove to heat the house, and every year we bought for the whole winter a truckful of coal. We had to schlep it in buckets to the basement bin. There was a Russian prisoner of war who worked for the coal delivery man, and someone had to wait with him while the coal was being delivered. So one time I did. There was a revolution going on in Budapest then. The people wore white marigolds and everyone was throwing them up into the air. The Russian prisoner, he said to me, 'You call this revolution? By us in Russia there was revolution! The blood was spilling in the streets!'" She laughed. "He was a Communist."

She gazed at the brownstones with affection, as if she had found herself on her old block in early twentieth century Budapest, then she put her hand on my elbow.

"World War I, that was a terrible war, terrible," she said. "My mother's cousin, Pfeifer Ignác, was a very famous scientist in Hungary. Once he was even invited to the United States to speak. He was at the university, and he also worked at Tungsram, the big company that was like General

Electric. He was director of research there." She lifted her chin. "He was so famous, visitors would not sit down in his office, out of respect."

I nodded.

"Ignác Pfeifer and his wife, Jolan, they had a wonderful son, Imre. I will never forget his beautiful face." She looked up at the sky and squeezed my elbow. "World War I came, and Ignác Pfeifer could send his son to a factory as an engineer. But Imre wanted to go and fight. Everybody did. Ignác Pfeifer said, 'If other people go to the front, he can go, too.' And what happened there?" she said with a knowing frown. "They were fighting the Russians, and both sides were in, they dug in the dirt, the—"

"The trenches?"

"Yes, yes, the trenches," she said. "One side would run at the other and many would die." She swept both hands to one side, then continued. "Imre had in his group a very good friend from Budapest. One time Imre realized that his friend was not there. Then they heard his friend screaming out in the middle of the battlefield. Nobody moved," she said in a whisper. "Ignác Pfeifer had paid money to an officer that he should protect Imre. But suddenly Imre jumped out of the bunker and crawled to his friend. 'You are surely an angel,' his friend said to him. The friend, he would have died anyway." She swatted her hand at an insect I could not see. She looked at me and shook her head. "Imre put him over his shoulder and ran for the trench. The Russians were shooting at him. The Hungarians were shooting back at the Russians." She gestured her arm forward as if pointing a rifle. "The first bullet hit him in the leg."

I winced.

"The second bullet, in the head. He died right there."

The vision of Imre and his friend lying bloodied on a rutted battlefield weighed on us, slowing our pace.

"His mother, Jolan, she nearly died, too, when she heard," my grandmother continued. "Terrible, terrible thing. She must have blamed her husband, that he didn't do something to keep her son home." Her face flushed. "At the end of her life she had to have a nurse twenty-four hours. I never forget it, Aunt Jolan sitting in a wheelchair, her tongue hanging out."

We stopped at Park Avenue. Prewar apartment buildings, looking freshly laundered and pressed, lined the wide, clean street. A neatly trimmed lawn and colorful tulips filled the median.

"It's kind of odd," I said, gesturing toward the flowers, "this and Aunt Jolan." She nodded and smiled. I thought about how frequently she recalled tragic circumstances, how enthusiastically — there was no better word for it — even as she decried them. Despite the pain, tragedy seemed to offer her rewards at least as rich as joy. The fabric of her being seemed woven with the two in equal measure. I did not welcome pain, and, for me, tragedy was something to be avoided at all costs, perhaps even at the cost of happiness.

We gazed down Park, then turned our faces to the sun, eyes closed, for a few long moments.

"There were two cousins of mine," she said brightly, seeming to sense my mood, "Simon and István."

"The ones the Nazis took?" I said.

Surprise interrupted her pleasant expression. "Yes, but this was many years before that." She took my arm and pulled me forward. "They lived in Nagykanizsa, that is west of Budapest, past Lake Balaton. The two of them, they looked like twins." She held up two fingers to make sure I understood. "One day, Simon decided to go to the barber in the town, the new barber, to shave off his beard."

"Simon, he had the motorcycle, right?"

"Yes," she said, "but this was after that." Then she smiled. "So he went into the shop, asked for a shave, and sat back in the chair. 'Take your time,' he said to the barber. The barber brushed the foam on his face. 'You have a very thick beard,' he told Simon. The barber shaved the beard with careful strokes of his blade, took a long time. He cleaned the blade, sharpened it again, cut the rest of the beard off. When he was done, the barber patted lotion on Simon's face. 'Now this is a shave,' the barber said. He was very proud of his work."

She stopped to take off her light jacket and fold it over her arm. "At home István admired Simon's shave." She studied my face as István might have. "'You are so clean and young looking,' he said to his brother. Then he winked and they both laughed."

"Why?" I asked.

She shook her head and continued, trying to contain a smile. "Now István, he walked down to the barber shop. He went in, but the barber was in the back. 'Hello?' István called. The barber appeared. He thought he was looking at the man he had just shaved, but with a full beard again!" She stopped and squealed a great, bouncy laugh. "'It is you!'" she said, her voice high, barely able to get the words out. "'But you were just here!'" Her eyes were wide with the barber's surprise.

Then she became István, rubbing her cheek and her chin and frowning as she wagged her finger at me.

"'This is what happens when you don't do a good job. It grows right back! Now let's try again!'" she said, emphasizing each word with a poke of her finger in my chest.

Her face drew up into a pink, wrinkly pucker as she chortled, and her eyes filled with tears from the pleasure of the memory. She gathered her breath with a chirping "*Jaj!*" wiped her eyes with a handkerchief, and kept laughing.

I savored the story as we turned down Ninetieth Street, oblivious at first to the flowering trees near the end of the block as we came upon them. Sunlight highlighted the blossoms and helped release their fragrance. My grandmother stopped in front of one of the trees and pulled down a low branch. She examined a cluster of flowers, touched them to her nose, and inhaled, drawing the rich scent into her body. "So beautiful," she said. She moved the branch over and held it for me, and the smell tingled the nerves in my head and softened the muscles in my back. I nodded in agreement. Then she released the branch and watched it settle back into place.

We re-entered the Y, squinting as our eyes adjusted to the relative darkness of the lobby. We were late and the classroom doors were closed. I opened one door and held it for her as she slipped into the room and found our seats. The lecturer was talking about Renaissance music. He paused, pressed a button on his tape player, and the room filled with a strange, soothing soprano. After a few minutes, I looked over at my grandmother. Her eyes were closed and her chin rested on her chest, rising slowly, falling slowly.

[18]

The wedding took place on a crisp and cloudless October Sunday. A Nor'easter had raged all the previous afternoon and evening, clearing the air. We gathered in the garden of an old historic house, under a chuppa, surrounded by a hundred-odd guests — friends, immediate family, cousins, and two ancient grandmothers, one from Ireland, one from Hungary. A justice of the peace led us through a Jewish-flavored ceremony. Two close friends read poems, another sang. I stomped on a glass wrapped in a cloth napkin, and a blanket of applause enwrapped us as Norah and I kissed.

Happy conversation filled the little ballroom set at the head of the garden, muffling the string trio that played in a corner. Tea sandwiches and cakes covered two tables, wildflowers springing from every inch of space between the tiered trays. I had envisioned a Saturday evening wedding, a sit-down meal, a band, a raucous hora. As we toured venues and talked through the details, however, something else began to take shape. Petulant and resistant at first, I opened myself to the possibilities. There was a moment during the afternoon when, gazing out the French doors, my eyes came to rest on the small fountain in the center of the garden lawn. Splotchy black lichen colonies grew on two weather-worn cherub statues. I experienced a feeling of great comfort and thought about how well the day fit me, how well it fit us. Letting go of how I thought things ought to be had made something wonderful possible. I had trusted to love. That was the way to take the step, I thought; the rest would work itself out in time.

Later I was sitting at a table talking with a group of people when I felt a hand on my shoulder. My grandmother. She wore a shiny lavender dress and carried a small black purse over her elbow. Her blond wig was full and neat. She was so short that when I looked over she was at eye level. A great smile brightened her face. I thought of Emery, and how hasty and administrative her marriage of necessity to him must have been, how different the circumstances. Then I thought of Alexander.

"Dear Peter," she said, holding my cheeks in her hands. "Good. So very good."

I grinned, and hugged her tight.

[19]

She got out less often in winter, as did I. Though I had observed that New Yorkers were essentially out-of-doors people, pushed out by small apartments, pulled out by stores, culture, parks, and friends, I also had discovered that in winter they tended to hibernate — snow, ice, and winter colds reducing the frequency and distance of their journeys. As they were fewer, winter outings seemed special. Shortly before Christmas, Norah and I splurged and treated my grandmother to tea at the Pierre Hotel, where we showed her our honeymoon photos. Later, in the cold of February, stirred by the lengthening light, we drove out to Queens and took her to a German restaurant for schnitzel.

She did not return to Hunter, but she did seem to steady over those months, to strengthen even. When the air began to warm, I arranged to meet her at MoMA. Arriving well ahead of time, I scanned the shifting, noisy crowd in the low-ceilinged lobby. A group of tourists encircled a well-dressed guide. A young bohemian couple held hands in a corner. Two older women in fur coats moved toward the exit with purpose. My grandmother stood near the entrance to the museum store. Her mouth sagged, her skin was dull, and she stared through the other visitors, rather than at them. Our eyes met and her face became taught and alive.

"*Szervusz*, Peter!" she said. "I have been here already since eleven o'clock."

"I am sorry, Granny," I said as I took her hands and kissed her on the cheek, "the one day I am early, I am late."

Her smile vanished. "They changed the guide, dear," she said in an exaggerated whine as she waved the museum events brochure at me. "I do not know what is here. What should we do?" She seemed beside herself and her anxiousness filled me.

"Okay, let's figure this out," I said, taking the program and trying to sound authoritative.

"What about this Chuck Close?" she said, starting off toward the escalator.

I had wanted to avoid the Close exhibit. Her hatred of postwar modern art was visceral and complete, and the prospect of Close brought to mind her reaction to the Jasper Johns retrospective we had once seen together. As we wandered through the Johns show, her obvious disgust built to outrage until she was unable to contain herself. Standing in front of a large gray canvas, rigid with distress, she had demanded of me and, through her volume, of the others in the room, "What is this? A broom?" I wilted from embarrassment. "Peter, why did he put a broom in the painting?" Her tone was declarative rather than inquisitive, and I knew that no explanation would satisfy.

We entered the gallery and paused in front of a study demonstrating Close's method. I whispered the written explanation to her as she stared at the deconstructed picture and braced myself for her reaction. "Unbelievable!" she exclaimed, turning a number of heads. Elated, she hurried from room to room, devouring the paintings. She admired them from afar and studied them up close, sharing her surprise at the subjects, her wonder at his technique. Close's work energized her, but by the time we reached the end, she looked tired, and she sat down on a bench and sighed. "My back bothers me," she said. "This has never happened to me before." She spoke in a low, weak tone as if talking to herself. We sat for a few minutes, lost in thought. Her gaze drifted around the room, then stopped at me. She smiled and nodded, then she stood up, letting out a muffled grunt as she did so. "Peter, tell me," she said, "you are not hungry?"

She placed a big chocolate brownie on my tray. "Take a brownie, too," she said. "You are so thin, and you are my guest today." We wound our way through the museum cafeteria and took what seemed to be the last unoccupied table, which overlooked the sculpture garden.

"So, I don't know about this job, Granny," I said, almost without thinking.

"Mmm?" she said over the top of her sandwich.

I wanted her guidance but did not know how to ask for it. "The travel is rough. Monday to Thursday, every week. I hate flying," I said, sadness stirring within me. "The work just isn't me. Cost reduction. The sharp point of the economic chisel. Anything a plant manager can do to cut cost, he must do. It's true that the factories are amazing, but the work is turning me into a person I do not like."

My grandmother did not take her eyes off mine. "What else would you do?"

"I don't know, maybe some writing," I said.

"Writing?" she said, curious.

"Yes. But that would depend on finding a way to make money that I enjoy. Writing won't pay the bills." I tried my best to sound as if I had a plan, some direction.

"That sounds very clear," she said.

"Maybe," I said.

She concentrated on her sandwich and then took a long drink of water. Her mind seemed to have moved on to something else and I was disappointed.

"You know," she said, still swallowing her food, "I was at your grandmother Rose's house many years ago. They invited us over to their house all the time. Her family was big and there were always many people there. It was nice that Rose and Rob included us.

"Anyway," she continued, "I did not know what to do and Rose's sister, that was Birdie, she told me I should go to work for the city. I never forget it. I passed both the city and the state exams for the civil service, but the city came first and so I took a payroll job with the hospitals. In my career I took seven exams, and I passed every one." She smiled with confidence. "The result of the last exam came after I was retired. I was seventy! They asked me to come to Worth Street. I told them I already retired, they didn't know!" She was laughing, then coughing.

"When was it that Birdie said that to you?" I said, diverted from my own quandary.

"I started with the city 1955."

"But you came in—"

"1950. January 1950.

"So what did you do after you arrived but before the city job? Were you home?"

"Agh," she said. "No. When I first got here, I found that Emery did not have a job, not for seven months." She held up three fingers. "He had not told me. He wanted me to go to work right away."

Her voice was tense, her posture hunched. I recalled the way I recoiled from Emery's affections when I was a boy. His physical presence was awkward — the droopy face accented by a bottom lip that turned out in a perpetual pout, clothed in baggy suits and too-wide ties. The cane he used to lever himself out of a chair he carried like a weapon. He spoke mostly in Hungarian, mostly to my grandmother, almost always arguing or complaining. He grabbed for the few hugs I gave him and held me roughly and with a kind of urgency. He was married to my grandmother, but I never thought of him as my grandfather.

"I went to Broadway with Emery and Irene, you know that is his sister, to look for work," she said after a sip of coffee. "We stopped in every store that was selling women's garments because that is what I knew. One store wanted me to be a fitter. But I did not speak any English, and I told

Emery I would not take the job because I could not understand the customers. He was very rude to me. He said to me in Hungarian, 'I will hit you on your ass if you don't take that job.' But I did not." She shrugged and chuckled. "The next day I went to the Joint Distribution Committee's employment office by City Hall. They gave me an address near where Lincoln Center is today. I thought it was not far from City Hall so I walked there. Can you imagine! It was afternoon by the time I got there!"

"It was garment work. I could do very nice handiwork, make beautiful button holes and everything, so the woman, Mrs. Stevens was her name, she took me. A few weeks later I heard that a cutter was going back to London. I had a very nice yellow silk two-piece dress from my store in Hungary, a skirt and a top," she said, touching her shoulders. "I showed it to Mrs. Stevens, and she said that if I would cut it now I would be her cutter. I made the pattern and cut it, but there was no one to sew it. So I had to stay until nine o'clock in the evening to sew the skirt. I couldn't work on an electric sewing machine, and I don't know how did I manage that I finished the skirt," she said, her eyes full of joy.

"Goodness, what did Emery say about being so late?" I said.

She nodded. "I was afraid of him, so I called Irene that she should tell him that I have to stay for a long time to finish the job. When I was done, I took the elevated train to the Bronx, and at around ten o'clock or so I arrived home. The light was on, I could see from the outside, but when I tried the door, it was locked. I rang the bell many times, but he did not let me in. So I went to his brother Alex who lived nearby. He was a very nice man. He came with me to Emery and somehow made him open the door."

I watched a group of Japanese tourists take photos of one another in the sculpture garden. It occurred to me that the fact that we spoke so little of Emery in the family might mean that there was a great deal to say. Yet a kind of dread enshrouded his name, and I half-hoped the subject would change.

"I got the job and I became the cutter and I was the happiest woman in the world!" she said, seeming not to notice my unease. "It was a very responsible job. Mrs. Stevens was very good to me, but she was a difficult woman. Sometimes she was very nice to people, other times she was very rude. There was such a nervous atmosphere in the workshop. I thought I could get a job elsewhere, so when I got my vacation I didn't go back. But then I found that everybody in the business cut with machines, not the old-fashioned way anymore, with scissors. Also, I couldn't speak Yiddish and that was a problem because at these factories that was the language the bosses spoke. God almighty!" she said, shaking her head, her hands on her cheeks. "I was out of work for a few weeks and I did not know what to do. Then Alex told me, 'Come to our store, be a saleslady.'"

"At the bakery?" I asked.

"Yes, Cakeland on 108th Street," she said, gesturing over my shoulder. "We moved to Queens around then."

"And how did that work out?" I said.

She snorted. "A very strange story. Louis, that is Irene's husband, he was the baker and Alex was the salesman in front. I don't know how it was, but Louis says, 'Maria, there is some money missing. You made some mistake with the money.' I told him, 'No, that is impossible, I am very, very careful with the money.'" She shook her head. "But I said I will work for that money. I don't know how many times the money was missing. Finally, after one and a half years I did the same thing that I did with Mrs. Stevens. After my vacation I left Emery, and I left the store."

"You left Emery?" I said, "You mean, you walked out?"

She stared down at her empty plate. "Emery was like hell," she said. "He knew I was working for his brother and brother-in-law at the bakery, and he thought he could do anything he wants." She squinted and slid her jaw forward. "I stayed in some kind of hotel, the Paris Hotel on West End Avenue and—"

"Ninety-Seventh Street?" I said. "That's right across from my apartment!"

"Yes, I was there maybe five weeks," she said. Absorbed in the past, she barely registered the coincidence. "I didn't dare look for another job because I was afraid that Emery would find me."

Learning that she had left him, even for a time, alleviated the gloom and tension I was experiencing, and I thought of her then. At some point she must have sat on one of those benches looking out upon the wide, gray Hudson and its treacherous currents, questioning her choices, fantasizing about returning to Hungary. But she was not one to wallow, and the scenes I envisioned shifted to walks to one of the movie theaters that then thrived in the neighborhood, a stop at the butcher, cooking a meal in her tiny rented room at the Paris, quiet nights mending an outfit, a murmuring radio for company. Perhaps there was a dream of a new life. Yet alone, out of work, with little English, she must have understood that she had few choices. I sensed her doubt and anger, her fear.

"I belonged to a union and the union man told me about a job at the Éclair Bakery on Seventy-Second and First Avenue, somewhere there," she said, looking both relieved and anxious, as she must have been then. "Eventually, I went there to work. The next day Emery was there."

I squeezed a shoulder toward the back of my neck. "The union man?"

"Yes, the union man told him." She paused, deflated. "At Éclair I was working for more than four years. Then I went to the city hospitals."

She glanced at her watch. I wanted her to stay with the memory a little longer.

"So, you went back," I said.

She gave a tiny nod, then she leaned back and looked at her watch again. It was an hour before the film in the theater downstairs. "Peter," she said, picking up her tray, "won't we be late for the movie?"

[20]

I opened the futon with a thud, flapped out the sheets, and made the bed. Over a late dinner at a nearby diner, we had spoken little other than to agree on the most important things we needed to deal with so that we could be done the next day. We were both exhausted. My father emerged from the bathroom dressed in his pajamas, medicine bag in one hand. He said a polite goodnight to Norah and then clambered into the futon-bed. He folded his hands on his chest, and he groaned a groan of physical fatigue, of mental depletion. At the same time, I knew that he was pleased at reaching a desired destination. He made that same sound when collapsing into bed after a long trip abroad with the senator. My sister and I would sit on the floor by the bed, examining and clutching the gifts he brought us, oddly clothed dolls, embroidered shirts, carved instruments. He would tell us a bit more about his trip, then wiggle into a comfortable position, close his eyes, and give a long sigh that said he was drained from the travel, but satisfied with his work, and unambiguously happy to be home with us. As I felt again the warmth and connection of those moments, I heard a contrast in the groan he had just given, a note of melancholy.

"I never hugged my mother," he said, eyes closed. "One time when I was saying goodbye to her at the bus terminal and I did not hug her, she said, 'One day you will be sorry.'"

He opened his eyes and smiled. "Thanks, Pete," he said. He lifted his forearm and we clasped hands. Then he lay his arms across his belly and within minutes he was asleep.

I cleared the dish drain as quietly as I could, then took the trash to the trash chute. I got ready for bed. Before turning out the light, I went to the bookcase and stared at the several books on Hungarian history and the Holocaust. The smooth bindings beckoned, and, as I stood there, I tried to marshal the energy to take down one of the volumes and read. Then tiredness brought on by the day's work and by the churning of unformed questions and doubt, mixed with my impulse to know, and my will failed. Only a diffuse, smoky desire remained.

"Bastard!" my father hissed as he pounded the steering wheel with his palm. He glared at the BMW streaking past us. "Look at him! So, I'm not going fast enough?" He pressed down on the gas pedal and we sped over the Triboro Bridge toward Queens.

"Dad," I said, trying to sound soothing as I gripped the door handle.

He shook his head. "People are just crazy. Crazy!"

I scanned upper Manhattan for the tall building across from my apartment and breathed in the fresh scent of the new car, a strangely pleasant combination of leather and plastic. The smell brought to mind a big Mercury Marquis we once had, and childhood road trips. My father often grew drowsy behind the wheel, even as he popped No-Doze pills like candy, and this made us all anxious. Sometimes he playfully exploited our fears by feigning sleepiness and complaining that if he only had a neck massage he would be fine. Then my sister and I would take turns squeezing his shoulders from the back seat until our fingers hurt. At night on two-lane roads he loved to play a game with us called The Lost Part, where he would turn off the headlights and accelerate into the pitch darkness until we shrieked in terror-stricken delight.

That morning I had considered offering to drive, but I knew how much he loved it, and I had hoped it might distract him from the unpleasantness of returning to his mother's apartment to finish the job. It had not occurred to me that the opposite might occur, that the task ahead might distract him from the driving needed to get there. I glanced at the passenger-side mirror and saw a van approaching. Our car started to drift left just as the van jumped to the left to pass us. On instinct, I reached over and grabbed the steering wheel to pull us back into our lane. My father stripped my hand from the wheel as he screamed, "Don't!" and our car weaved back and forth.

"You were going to hit that car," I shouted, pointing out the window. The van passed us, the man in the passenger seat glaring as he streaked by.

"I was not," my father yelled, spitting the words, his face red.

"Yes, you were, Dad," I said, with a nervous chuckle.

"Don't laugh at me! It's not funny! The jerk."

"Dad," I said, quieter, plaintive, my heart pounding.

"Don't Dad me," he muttered.

I gazed out the window at a plane landing at LaGuardia. The old World's Fair towers came into view. "Here, it's coming up on the right, the exit for 108th Street," I said softly.

"Where? Oh, there," he said, with appreciation. He flicked on the blinker and turned his head to check the adjacent lanes.

The place was a mess, and it felt smaller and more cramped than the previous day. The many half-filled bags of giveaway items and trash had turned the living and dining rooms into an obstacle course. The nails and hooks that only hours before had held artwork and family pictures formed an irregular pattern on the walls, like the first drops of rain on dry pavement or a spattering of bullets. Next to the doorway that led to the bathroom and study was a cushioned chair. On the chair sat the small box of things my father and I were collecting to take with us: a plastic bag with the old documents, the photo album from before the war, a silver serving tray, the Herendi plate that bore the image of my great grandfather, her notebooks. Next to the chair was the antique desk. The orange-brown grain of the old wood seemed to shimmer.

"Good morning, dear Peter," said my aunt. She wore a beige outfit that blended with the color of the walls, and I had not noticed her as I stepped into the apartment. She was standing at the dining table, sorting the china. After greeting us, she gave a loud, heavy exhale. "I do not know how we will finish today," she said. "Is your father here? Danicom?" she shouted toward the front door, "I have a question for you."

"He's parking the car," I said.

"Could you help me here, Peter honey? Irene is coming to look at the dining table and I want to clear off all this stuff." She put the collection of Herendi china bells into one of the boxes of things she was planning to take with her. "I will keep them in our garage," she said. "Your father said they would not fit in the car."

My father stopped in the front doorway and surveyed the room. "All right," he said to us, resigned, then he disappeared into the back.

I helped Eve load the bells and sort the rest of the plates and dishes from the china cabinet. "Maybe your mother or your sister would want these," she said, passing her hand over several ordinary-looking serving dishes.

"I don't know," I said, looking around for something else to do. I wandered over to the closet and touched the sleeve of a blazer, one of the few outfits that had survived the giveaway pile.

"She made that, you know," said Eve.

I nodded.

"In Hungary she was a master ladies' tailor."

"She was always fixing our clothes," I said, stroking the fabric, recalling evenings during visits to Maryland when we would sit and watch television and my grandmother would hem a skirt of my mother's or patch a worn pair of my jeans. With her eyeglasses looking as if they might slip off the end of her nose, pins poking from between her lips, thimble on one finger, she worked rapidly in between catnaps.

"Did you know she had a store in the very elegant part of Budapest?"

I did, but I shook my head anyway.

"A women's fabric store, Nivo, it was called," she said, leaning forward. "A lovely store on the Vaci utca. Actually, a side street, even better than the Vaci utca. Retail, no bigger than this room. There was a glass enclosure in front with all the fabrics. Good stuff. It had to be good in that neighborhood. Upstairs there was a salon where she made dresses. She ran it with two other women, very sophisticated Jewish women. She was in the store all the time, never home. Grandmother did all the cooking, though there was a maid, too. I was complaining that she was not around enough."

Eve pouted coolly.

"Thinking about it later, I knew she had a big responsibility. She paid the tuition and supported us. She just couldn't be a mother. I wanted to go to dancing school, social dancing. She didn't want to let me because God forbid I would meet a boy. She was afraid. I was boy crazy and I don't blame her." She chuckled. "But my aunt talked her into it."

I felt the rough weave of the blazer again, then sat down at the antique desk and shuffled through some papers.

"Then somehow this English teacher appeared. Tall guy, older, maybe forty, with one glass eye and a toupee. He was a spy for the English in Hungary and he stayed after the war. He knew what was happening with the Communists and he wanted to marry me and get me out. But it didn't happen," she said, tilting her head as if mocking herself, "obviously. Dani, he was allowed to do everything, but me, at nineteen, I still had pigtails. And one day you know what I did? I cut the pigtails in the morning and I flushed them down the toilet," she laughed, "so she could not glue them back!"

She was quiet for a moment.

"I don't think she liked me," she said, her voice low and raspy. "I'm not blaming her," she added in her mother's defense, or her own. It was difficult to tell. "We just didn't have a relationship. You know how sometimes there's no chemistry? But my aunt Jancsi, she accepted me with open arms." She smiled. "I would go next door to her apartment and take a bath, and after my bath I would curl up in this overstuffed armchair. Jancsi *néni* would settle herself on the big couch in front of the samovar, always a cup of tea in her hands. 'Tell me,' she would say to me. I was in this wonderful high school where everybody was happy. Before, they didn't like Jews in the school, now it was fine. I had all these girlfriends. I was in love with the principal, a gorgeous priest. I was delirious."

She clutched her chest.

"It was a semblance of security and structure like I used to know when my father was alive. I was full of stories and nobody to tell except Jancsi *néni*. My mother was so jealous of Jancsi. I'm sure it caused her a lot of pain. One time I told her, 'You don't listen to my stories.' And you know what she said? 'I feed you, I clothe you, and that's all I owe you.'"

She stared at me as if waiting for me to choose sides, hers or my grandmother's, her point of view or my own. I averted my eyes. For a moment I saw things as she did and appreciated the hurt she must have experienced, her beloved father dead, her distant mother too busy to comfort, to love. But confused and feeling I had betrayed something of my grandmother, I quickly withdrew from empathy, assuring myself that tenderness from my grandmother was more likely to have fueled Eve's teenage provocations than to have soothed them.

"So she was working long hours?" I said.

"She didn't have to say it like that," she said. "I can understand what she said, 'I can't do more, I give you what I owe you.' But it was cruel anyway."

Eve stood up and wound her way toward the back room.

"Dani?" she called.

Irene stopped by with her daughter at ten o'clock. She stepped with exaggerated care around the trash bags, more out of silent disapproval of the disorder than caution. She inspected the dining table, her big gray eyes glassy with indifference, an impression strengthened by her loose, red eyelids and thin nose. Her daughter stood behind her, peering over one shoulder, then the other, with glances that bounced between each of us, the back of her mother's neck, and the table.

Irene gave the table a tug to test how easily it opened, and it wobbled. She slid her fingers along one edge, and as she did so, I studied the light brown age spots on the back of her hand, the embroidery on the sleeve of her white knit cardigan. By the fact of my grandmother's marriage to her brother Emery, she was my great aunt, but she was never much in my life. From my father, I had learned that she had come into money some years back but remained as penny-pinching as ever. She was friendly with my grandmother—after all, she was the one who went to the apartment the day of the stroke—yet she had done little to help her over the years. She stopped at a chip in one corner of the table and rubbed her fingertips back and forth over it. She lifted her head slowly and looked at my father, then Eve. "How about a hundred dollars?" she said.

"A hundred dollars, mother?" blurted her daughter. "This is junk, it's worthless. Taking it for nothing would be doing them a favor."

Irene tilted her head, weighing the opinion, in the moments before my father exploded.

"Favor?" he said, slamming his fist on the table. "I'd rather chop it up and burn it, you cheapskate!"

"Dani!" Eve said. "Irene is—"

"My mother was a martyr," he said, jabbing a finger at Irene, "taking that basket case Emery off your hands."

"Dani, please," said Irene. Her voice sounded meek, but her eyes were hard. She flicked her wrist. "We did what we could."

"What you could?" shouted my father. "When your brother Alex died, when your sister Margaret died, Emery's brother and sister, was there a dime for my mother? After what she did for you, for all of you? No! You kept it all." He pointed at her again, even as his rage began to exhaust itself. "You kept it," he said.

"But Dani," Irene said with a faint note of disdain, "it was not as if — " She stopped, and for a minute no one said a word. Irene's pale, bony fingers fastened a single button on her sweater. Then she turned to her daughter and nodded, and without another word, the two of them left.

[22]

She stood in front of MoMA looking frantic. "It is Wednesday, and they are closed Wednesdays. How do I not remember this?" she said, her eyebrows bent with distress, her voice shaking.

I did not respond at first, expecting that any moment her despair would pass and she would assign us a plan. But as the seconds stretched and her pleading expression did not change, taking charge felt unavoidable. Uncomfortable with this role, I struggled to think of an alternative. Then the obvious flashed into my mind.

"No problem," I said, now buoyant, taking her hand. "Let's go to the Metropolitan."

We boarded an uptown bus, and in a short while we were settled in for lunch in the Met's cafeteria.

"I left the job. I've been doing some writing, but it is not going well." I figured it was better this way, telling her up front and straight rather than waiting for her to ask how I was doing.

"Oh?" she said, sipping her soup and frowning.

"I have been at it for a few months and have nothing to show for it. It's not good."

She nodded as she slurped. A surge of shame filled me.

"I did get my first consulting project, though," I said.

"Mmm?" she said.

"It's just about done."

I took a few large bites from my slice of pizza. She finished her soup.

"And what does Norah say?" she asked.

I hesitated.

"She doesn't say much," I said. Out of the corner of my eye I caught sharp glances from two older women at the table next to us. I shifted in my seat and tried to concentrate. "I like writing, but I need to make more money."

She smiled at me, reached across the table, and patted my hand.

"There are a few more possible consulting projects," I said, trying to sound definite. But the truth was things did not look even as good as that.

"And how is dear Norah?" she said.

"Good. She got a raise."

"Wonderful!" she said.

"She is working very hard now, the last couple of weekends even," I said. "I have a lot of dreams, Granny, things I want to do. How do I live them when there are so many reasons not to?"

I needed her strength, her certainty. I wanted her to tell me what to do, but she only stared out over my shoulder, cloudy-eyed.

"I am sorry I can no longer go to the Hunter College," she said. "The subway is too much, everybody pushing."

"Why don't you look for something in the middle of the day?" I said. "We had that nice class at the Y."

"Do you know how old I am?" she asked.

"Yes, of course!" I said.

I felt disappointed at having received no response from her, no guidance, and then I understood that we cannot be decided for, we cannot attain hope and direction by transplant. *Yet we can listen*, I thought. And though this did not comfort me much, I felt less pain somehow.

After working our way through a lacquer exhibit, we sat on some stools to rest. She let out a short hiss when we stood up. "My back," she said, reaching around to her lower spine. "Aching." She shook her head and picked up her purse. Then she said, as if to herself, "As long as I can walk, it will be okay."

I tried to think of something encouraging to say to her.

"I wonder if there is a bathroom near here," she said, as she started walking toward the doorway.

Later we tried to find the Korean prints and wandered into a great hall dominated by a huge Asian-themed fresco and a giant, exotic statue. She made a beeline for a long bench in the middle of the room, while I retrieved a diagram from a box next to the fresco.

"That is Bhaishajyaguru," I said, nodding toward the large figure in a red robe at the center of the faded work. "He is the Buddha of medicine."

"Yes," she said, her eyes darting around the fresco, "it is so intricate. Who are those people there?"

"By his knees?"

"Yes."

I scanned the diagram. "In the yellow pants, he is a secondary bodhisattva, carrying a medicine bowl. The other is carrying a monk's staff."

"Mmm, that group of men back there?" she said, wriggling her finger at the left side.

"'Guardian generals,'" I read, "'they personify Bhaishajyaguru's vows to help the needy by curing illness, providing clothing and other necessities, and ensuring the birth of healthy children.'"

"And look up there," she said, smiling at a small figure near the top of the fresco, "she is floating on a cloud in the sky." She shook her head in wonder. "Where was this from?"

"A temple in North China, from the early 1300s."

"*Jaj*!" she said, rocking back and forth.

We talked about the piece for a long time, then just sat and studied it. She searched the fresco as if in a trance, her face calm but for the slightly upturned corner of her mouth. She turned to me. "It is possible always to discover new things," she said. "Wonderful." Then she absorbed herself again in the art. The room was bright, the air itself nearly glistening. Several people walked up and down the ramp at the far end of the hall on their way to and from other galleries. To our right was the massive statue, a god-like figure that looked down upon us with a soft, expectant expression, its thin eyes topped by arched eyebrows, its lips gentle and flowing. I walked over and read the plaque next to it, then returned.

"The fresco is from the 1300s, and the statue," I said, turning toward it, "the statue is from the five hundreds. The statue is almost eight hundred years older than the fresco." I felt amazement light up my face. "Eight hundred years older!"

My grandmother's eyes widened and she touched the side of her cheek. We meditated on the fresco and the statue, soaking in the idea of how many years, how many lifetimes, had passed since the last chisel, the last brush, touched these works.

She took my arm as we started down the museum's front steps, weaving our way through the clusters of people soothing themselves in the midafternoon June sun. I put my hand on hers and watched to make sure she did not misstep. She is getting old, I thought to myself, and then it occurred to me that neither of us had raised the subject of family history all day.

"What do you think about this gay thing?" she said out of the blue.

Knowing how conservative her politics were, I selected careful words. "Well, I'm not really for it, but I'm not against it," I said. "People choose."

I braced myself for an impassioned rehash of some article she had read in the *Post* that morning, but she just nodded. A woman watched her two children chase one another in circles near the south fountain. We passed a long line of people waiting to buy sodas and ice cream from a pushcart.

"Saturday I leave for the Poconos with the Elder Hostel," she said.

"Oh, that's nice," I said. "The usual group?"

"Yes, the same. After that, I go to your parents, to Washington."

She needed quarters for the bus, and I stopped to ask a young couple to change a dollar.

"When will I see you?" she asked.

"Maybe I'll come down to D.C. when you're visiting Mom and Dad," I said. "If not, we'll do something here just after."

Horns blew from somewhere on Fifth Avenue, and I wondered about her trip home. A bus down Fifth, then the subway to Queens, then another bus, I guessed. It would take an hour and a half, maybe. I began to worry about her, but reassured myself that taking public transit was as easy and reflexive as breathing for her. She had made the trip thousands of times. Yet this effort at restoring the image of her as strong and self-sufficient faltered, and for an instant I pictured her at home that evening, eating a simple dinner in front of the television in the mostly dark apartment, alone. How did loneliness not overwhelm her? I wondered. I wished for a way to ease it, and when none came to mind, I resolved to do more for her come fall, to take more responsibility. I started to say something, then I stopped. A breeze spread the sweet smell of chestnut trees over us, and I drew a deep breath. I looked at her, aware of how strongly I felt toward her, aware of how childhood affection, which became reflexive as I grew up and my world filled with girls and college and travel and work, and might have stayed a stale habit, had transformed over the years of our visits into love. I sniffed the chestnut trees again and for a moment I was satisfied, appreciating how we had captured the elusive chance for friendship.

She smiled at me and we held hands. The bus arrived, she hustled toward the door, and there was little time to say goodbye. I kissed her on both cheeks. "I will call you in a week, after you are back from the Poconos," I said, hugging her tightly. Then the bus swallowed her up.

[23]

Late morning, a truck arrived from a charity for Jewish immigrants, and three beefy Russians started to remove the unwanted furniture from the apartment. They carried out lamps and the coffee table and set them at the curb behind the truck. They carried out chairs and boxes of unwanted glasses and pots. I worked on getting the sagging bookcases ready for them, sweeping armfuls of *Reader's Digest* collections and condensations from the shelves and stacking them in piles on the floor. The picture of my grandmother in the old photo album came to mind, the one where she was sitting up in bed holding an open book. It had been a surprising sight, because I could not recall ever having seen her reading during visits to our house. She kept up with the day's news and delved into the college classes she audited, but fundamentally she was a woman of action. That she had read Churchill's six-volume history of the Second World War, which I found on a top shelf, seemed only remotely possible. When the bookcases were empty, two Russians grabbed them and lugged them away.

Material flowed from the apartment like water down a bathtub drain. I watched the men take the ficus plant, the dictionary stand, and the china cabinet. The living room sofa stayed; a friend of Eve's was coming for it later. One of the crew who could speak a few words of English asked my father if he could have the VCR, and my father took it up with Eve. I went back to the study. The only thing left in the room was a faded gold, fifties-style couch. I pulled off the rough, square seat cushions and found two long, stiff pieces of cardboard underneath. I puzzled over this discovery for a moment, wondering whether it was some kind of odd storage place for recycling. The length and rigidity of the corrugated suggested a support function, and I realized that, at least in recent decades, she had slept there, on the sofa. I pushed away the sadness this Spartan habit aroused. But I could summon no memory of a bedroom or a bed from my few childhood visits. If there had been a bed, and I reassured myself that there must have been, when was it removed? And why? I imagined my grandmother having it taken away upon Emery's death. Yet, if this were the case, I reasoned, then she had spent some two decades sleeping on the back-room sofa. I felt the sadness reassert itself. Sleeping on a sofa for twenty years, as compared to a bed, involved a considerable sacrifice of physical comfort, and her choice offered a measure of her antipathy for Emery, an indication of his awfulness. Yet there also was strength and liberation in her action, and I saw the sofa as a symbol of bliss, too.

"Dad?" I said, drifting out to the living room.

"He's outside," Eve said, inclining her head toward the door.

"Granny, did she...." I said.

"Here, Peter, I want to show you this," she said, waving a *New York Post* she had pulled from the newspaper pile. I caught something in the headline about welfare cheats. "You see," she said, eyebrows raised, "we're moving toward the left, but people are not aware of it because the stock market is good."

I had no idea what she was talking about.

She leaned toward me. "We're not paying attention because we're historically dumbed down," she said, emphasizing each word. "It's just like in Hungary after the war. They took a grip, they had a plan. They called it 'social democracy.'" Sarcasm coated the phrase. "This was the plan, to stupefy everybody."

Her gaze was penetrating, challenging. At first I thought she was just taking a frustrated swipe at Bill Clinton, whom she hated. Then it seemed that maybe she was after something else.

"But the Russian Army was there, what did people expect?" I said, lowering my voice as one of the Russians walked in, picked up an end table, and walked out.

"Hungary was a royalty, always dealt with the West. What did we know about Communism?" she said, not caring who heard her. "If you make it a social democracy, nobody's going to rise up. Communism? That's in Russia." She was disgusted. "We were part of the Austro-Hungarian Empire, the Habsburgs. What did we have to do with Russia? 'Those are lower kind of people,' we Hungarians always said."

Another Russian emerged from the back room holding a little stool. He looked at Eve, she stared back, and he kept moving toward the front door. She had been so self-assured all through the previous day and this morning, but now she seemed tired, her expression bland, her shoulders curved, the burden of the clean-out and the surfacing of long-buried feelings weighing on her.

"It got bad after we left," she said. "They brought in peasants and re-educated them. Teachers were trained in six months. And if you were middle-class, you couldn't go to college. Kids were taught to report on their parents. You didn't have to prove anything. Nobody went to sleep before one o'clock in the morning. If the truck didn't come to take you away, you could go to sleep."

I thought of the sofa again. It was penitentiary-like. Yet in the light of Eve's story, I also saw how, when my grandmother considered what she had left in Hungary, when she compared life here to the conditions from which she had spared her children, she might have laid upon the makeshift bed with greater satisfaction.

I followed the Russians to the back room. They lifted the old couch and started to move it into the small hallway, but it became wedged in the door. The Russians backed up and tried it sideways, then they flipped the couch over and tried again. Each time the legs got stuck in the door frame, as if clutching it. The Russians muttered. Their faces grew red and sweaty. My father showed up and talked with the men. Then he took down the chandelier in the hall so they could try to ease the couch out standing on its side. No luck. They removed the sliding doors from the hall closet to make more room for maneuvering. It still was not enough. We all looked at the back window and then at the couch, shaking our heads in acknowledgment that the window was too small. The Russians tried to get the couch into the hall one last time, grunting as they jiggled it roughly back and forth, but it would not yield. As I watched, I imagined telling my grandmother the saga of the stubborn sofa, and I could almost hear her convulsive laughter. The men exhaled, shrugged, and left the couch in the study.

[24]

I took a seat in a chair beside the lone empty bed in the critical care room. The shades were down, and bed curtains diffused the little light that seeped through. By the window lay a large, older white man, his eyes closed, his feet hanging heavily off the end of his mattress. His wife sat beside him. The person across from them was invisible behind closed curtains. Next to me, near the door, was an elderly black woman. A younger woman, whom I judged to be the daughter, sat by her bed as she slept, attentive yet relaxed. When the old woman awoke, she murmured prayers with a minister who arrived with a bundle of flowers.

A bank of winking monitors, each beeping at a different interval and pitch, dominated the center of the room. I concentrated on the varying tones and rhythms as I watched the nurses, dark black women in white shirts and pants, dart between the monitors and patients down nearby halls. A deep wave of terror inside me was held as motionless as a specimen in amber by an even stronger numbing impulse. This suspension helped foster the sensation that I was floating above the situation I was now in, though the sensation did not last, as a powerful smell — a combination of disinfectant, urine, and the odor of sick bodies — bound me again to the fact that I was in a hospital.

There was a commotion behind me as red-smocked orderlies wheeled in another patient. She lay horizontal, her head resting on a thin pillow, a sheet covering her from the stomach down. She wore a light blue hospital gown, and her arms were straight and slack at her sides. Her face looked swollen, but I told myself that this might have been an illusion caused by the absence of her wig. Only a thin veil of tousled white hair covered her head. Her eyes were closed, and her chest rose and fell in slow, regular contractions. I stood at the side of the bed and stroked her arm. After a few minutes she opened her eyes and looked at me.

"*Egészségedre*, Peter," she said weakly.

"Just try and rest, Granny," I said. "It's okay. I am here and my father is flying up. He won't be long."

She nodded and closed her eyes.

A nurse appeared in front of me, a perky young woman with a pinned-on smile. She pressed a clipboard into my chest. "Are you Maria's son?"

"No, I'm her grandson," I said, taking a half step backward. "My father will be here soon."

"Okay, because we have some forms we will need you to fill out," she said, still holding out the clipboard. I glanced down at the papers, but I did not take them from her. The smile dropped from her face. "Or him," she said, and then she hurried off.

I sat down. After a few minutes I noticed that Granny was tapping her right hand on the mattress. Soon she began shaking her right leg. Her eyes were closed, but she seemed to be trying to communicate with me. I leaned over the bed, "Granny, are you all right?" I said. She did not reply, and the tapping did not cease. In another minute I raised my voice and repeated the question. "Granny, are you all right?"

She opened her eyes, then closed them. "I have," she slurred, and hearing herself, she stopped. She lay still for a few moments, then tried again. "I have to make," she said, resuming the tapping.

My stomach tightened and my mind emptied. "I'll be right back," I said, and I went in search of a nurse. The hallways were deserted, however, and I returned and stood by the door. I intercepted a nurse as she entered the room. She pressed a button to call an orderly. Five minutes passed. Granny shook her leg. I peered into the hallway for the nurse, an orderly, someone.

"Wet," she said. "Wet," louder now. She clenched her eyes.

I found another nurse and blocked her way. "Please," I said, my voice unsteady, "my grandmother." I forced the words out. "She has to urinate, I mean, I think she already has."

"We're doing what we can," the nurse said automatically. Then she looked at my grandmother again, then at me. "I'll get an orderly."

"It will be a few minutes, Granny," I said, touching her arm. "Not too long."

Finally, the orderly arrived, smiled, and, drawing the curtain, asked me to wait outside. A short while later the curtains squeaked open. Granny rested. I sat in the chair, dazed. My father had phoned me two hours earlier. She had had a stroke and was being transferred to Mount Sinai from North Shore Hospital. Could I go over until he got there? It seemed like days ago.

Soon she started tapping her fingers again and bouncing her knee. I studied the other patients in the room, trying not to notice her need. I had the urge to leave. Finally, I said, "Do you have to go again?" She nodded, and I told the nurse, who paused, glanced at my grandmother, and clicked her cheek before calling an orderly. We waited. Granny's face grew taut and she turned and looked at me through the bars of the bed, "Must ... hold ... it ... in," she whispered from her gut. "Must ... hold ... it ... in."

I went to find someone, but it was dinnertime and the orderlies were distributing food trays. I circled the floor and was about to walk the halls again when an aide materialized in front of her room.

We left the hospital late that night, and I took my father to dinner at an Indian place in my neighborhood that was still open.

"I can't believe it," he kept saying through mouthfuls of tandoori and naan. He looked shaken, exhausted. "She was just in Washington last week, taking the subway to museums, her usual tour." The meal soothed him, his mind settled, and soon he was telling me about his week and my mother's latest projects. Then we walked back to my apartment in the warm August night.

[25]

A small crowd surrounded Granny's bed the next day. My aunt Eve, uncle Ed, and cousin Julie had driven in from Westchester. My father, Norah, and I came from across the park.

"Where am I?" she said, her words slow and hoarse. "What am I doing here?"

My father pulled up a chair and spoke with her. "You had a stroke, mother," he said. "It seems that it has affected your left side. This is the hospital. They brought you here yesterday."

"Oh," she said, in a tone that suggested that she understood him only partially.

After massaging her left hand with her right, she tried to make a fist, but the fingers achieved only a loose curl. Everyone watched as she began to raise her left arm. It responded hesitantly, like a power lifter's barbell, and the wrinkles on her face deepened as she strained, willing it higher. When her wrist reached her forehead, she exhaled and lowered her arm to her lap. We all cheered and she smiled, the left corner of her lips sagging below the right side, turning the smile into a smirk.

"A physical therapist is coming later to help," said my uncle. *She can do this*, I thought. *We can help her do this.*

My father had brought a stack of postcards of Granny's favorite Impressionist paintings, hoping to provide her with a diversion, and he placed them in a neat pile in her lap. She steadied the pile with her weak left hand and picked up the first card with her right. She studied it at length but said nothing, and her eyes were empty, as if the card were blank. She turned it over and read the back. "Argenteuil. Claude Monet. Monet," she said, shaping the sounds with her mouth, as if saying the words for the first time. She picked up the next card, "Degas. Degas." She worked her way through the whole stack, neither perturbed nor amused, just faintly glad to have something to do. I sat and watched her. I had never seen her without her dentures, without her wig, and, even as the names of the artists stirred thoughts of the two of us strolling through the Met's Impressionist galleries — or perhaps because of this — I became convinced that the swollen-faced, thin-haired, toothless woman in the hospital bed in front of me was some stranger, not her.

Norah went out and soon returned with a vase of flowers. I showed them to Granny, and she looked up at me and smiled. Our eyes met, and I felt a deep contact with her that warmed me. I brought the bouquet close to her face, and she closed her eyes and inhaled once, then again. Her posture became less rigid. I turned the vase and she repeated long, sharp breaths—slow suction up the nose, then a quick puff out the mouth—as if trying to bring every sweet molecule of aroma from each bloom into her body. She paused. "Wonderful," she said, then she rested.

That evening we all gathered in the hallway outside Granny's room for a meeting with her doctor. He wore a Hawaiian shirt, khakis, and loafers, no socks. He sat back in a chair and put his feet up on the empty desk in front of him. "The CAT scan looks okay," he said, smiling through a deep tan. "It could have been much worse." We asked questions. What caused the stroke? How bad is the damage? How much will she recover? The information he offered was vague, yet somehow positive. Then he stood up. "She was in excellent physical condition. I expect she will recover enough to go back to her apartment and take care of herself. But let's see what happens over the next several days," he said, still grinning.

[26]

Midweek, Norah and I stopped by the hospital between work and dinner with friends. Norah took some remover and nail polish from her backpack, held Granny's left hand in her palm, and began to clean the dull, chipped fingernails. We talked about our plans for the weekend. Granny was more alert, and her left arm had regained some strength. After the nails on her left hand were done, she lifted the arm and moved it in little circles. Norah went over to the right side, squeezed Granny's hand, then rubbed the old polish from her nails. A calmness enveloped the room as Granny and I observed the work. I studied the aged fingers and noticed how they tapered from thick and fleshy at the palm to near points at the tips. Wrinkles gathered in thick folds around the knuckles. The skin was shiny. As the new polish was applied, I thought the hand became younger. When Norah finished, we all nodded with satisfaction.

Eve's other daughter, my cousin Janet, had flown in from Seattle the day before to visit the hospital, and we talked about her. "Janet looks good," Granny said, speaking deliberately, as if pounding out the words on an old typewriter, "better than before." She glanced at the doorway. "But don't tell anyone I said that." She laughed.

Then her expression grew serious. "I do not speak so well as I used to," she said.

"No," I said, "But it is better, and you look healthier." I touched her shoulder.

She looked down at her nails then at Norah. "Thank you," she said, channeling extra energy to the muscles around her mouth to make sure she was understood. "You are an angel."

It was time to go and we packed up our things. "I'll be back tomorrow at around 11:30."

"11:30 tomorrow?"

"Yes," I said from the doorway.

"I can hardly wait," she said as she closed her eyes.

[27]

My father made a jovial announcement. "The bathroom is empty, and the hall closet and the back room, mostly."

"What about the dining table, Dani?" said Eve. "If we're not selling it to Irene, what do we do with it?"

"Ugh," he said, the manic expression vanishing from his face, "I don't know." He sat down.

He was doing the best he could, and I felt both sadness and affection for him. "I'm hungry," I said. "Want to come with me to get sandwiches? It's almost lunchtime."

He rose instantly and followed me.

"What were you talking about with Eve earlier?" he asked me out on the sidewalk.

"Oh, I don't know," I said. "She was giving me a lecture about welfare and the Communists taking over Hungary."

"Mmm," he said, and we walked toward 108th Street. "I remember after the war I had a teacher who was a Nazi and then became a vociferous Communist," he said. "I argued with him about politics. That was not such a good idea." He shook his head. "Some days I didn't feel like going to school. I had this close friend and I just went to his apartment. His mother would sign some kind of phony absentee card, which I handed in the next day."

"Truant, huh?" I said, slapping him on the back.

"Nah, I was basically a good boy," he said, earnestly, but with a trace of regret. "I was involved with a youth group led by this young priest. We used to put on puppet shows."

"For kids?"

"Yes," he said. "There was a lot of hanky-panky going on between the boys and girls in the group. I fell madly in love with this girl, sent her notes every day. I couldn't wait to get notes back."

His eyes were shiny. "Through the priest I became one of the acolytes at St. Stephen's Basilica. It was the largest church in Budapest." He offered the detail as if he were quoting from a guidebook, sounding both proud and self-mocking.

I frowned.

"An altar boy," he said, sensing I had not understood. "Dressed in the priestly garments. A long black robe down to my feet, and a white smock over it. I carried the incense."

"Impressive," I said, complimenting him, but the idea rattled me. I considered the notion that he had been raised as a Catholic. He was a child, so my thinking went, the aunts were a strong influence, he was dragged there. But serving in the ceremonies demolished the belief that perhaps somewhere he had resisted, that he had adopted the appearance but not the conviction. I felt disturbed and distant and yet also fascinated.

"High Mass?" was all I could think to say.

"Yes, every Sunday. The priest would be up there, and I would kneel. The orchestra would play, and the choir would sing." He was staring straight ahead, and his voice was almost monotonous. "We knew the organist."

"Was it full," I asked, "the church?"

"Pretty full, maybe. But midnight mass during Christmas, completely full," he said, waving his hand out over the imaginary crowd.

"Did you serve then?"

"Oh, yeah, sure," he said, nodding. My ear caught the slight shuffle of his shoes against the sidewalk, which sounded like sandpaper on wood, and the gentle rhythm distracted me. He took my elbow. "You have to imagine. A young boy, singing, choir, orchestra, it was an intense religious experience for me, very personal."

"More than just liking the music?"

He glanced at me. "The music, the smells, the glittering costumes of the priest, everything together, it was glorious," he said. He looked out again at some unseen vision, his gaze intensifying. "I have never been so deeply, so religiously in love with God as I was during that period. Delirious." He savored the word and shook his head. "I never captured that same feeling as a Jew. Never."

I studied the pavement as we walked along. In parts the sidewalk had been cracked by the roots of the old trees that had forced their way through what was, ultimately, a weak and temporary barrier. His passion for his Catholic experience made him seem like a stranger. Then, I had a fleeting sense of myself as a stranger, and I felt close to him in a new way, identified with him. In that moment, I saw the barrier that had separated me from my father's youth, and how he had willed it into place, thick and solid, to block his fears, his guilt. Against this buttress, I reflected, I had built a barrier of my own. I had never told my father what my grandmother had said about the loss of family and friends during the war. I had never thought to. Now I understood that the effect of his silence about that period of his life was not neutral; it imparted to me an instinct to hide things. Reflexively, what my grandmother and I discussed I treated as a secret. But the revelations and confessions of the last day and a half had struck blows against the old barriers, leaving cracks and breaks.

"When did you first think of yourself as a Holocaust survivor?" I asked, focused on the concrete just ahead of my feet.

He looked up at the sky. "Well," he said, "I started getting letters from the Holocaust Museum in Washington. They considered me a survivor because I had lived through the war in Budapest. I got to go to the front of the line and didn't have to pay." He stopped and let go of my arm. "Real Holocaust survivors are people who survived the concentration camps." His face was firm and he spoke as if scolding himself. "When I was a kid, and when I was in Vienna, New York, and Washington, I never thought of myself as a Holocaust survivor."

I rubbed his back and took his arm. We passed a row of attached brick houses, matchbox-sized, but neatly kept. Two South Asian children played in a front yard. "Well, you didn't have much of a Jewish consciousness," I said.

"Zero."

We neared 108th Street. I felt confused, at once a child, wondering whether my father was for me or against me, and an adult, noting the link in our blurred senses of identity.

"Are you glad you're Jewish?" I asked.

"Oh, yes, absolutely," he said, sensing my struggle. "But you know, if I didn't meet Mom, I don't know what would have happened. Her family was really Jewish. Though I was not happy with my Catholic experience. It was completely unnatural."

"What do you mean?"

"Catholic doctrine damaged me, my outlook," he said, scanning the shops as we reached the corner. "In the refugee camp in Vienna, I hung out with a group of guys. A lot of them were Jewish and they had this fraternity-brother kind of attitude. They asked me if I had ever slept with a girl. I had not. One time I went with them to visit friends of theirs in a sanatorium outside the city. Turned out there was a girl there they wanted to fix me up with. 'Take care of this innocent, virgin boy,'" he said, echoing one of the gang. I nodded and gestured toward a sandwich place across the street.

"I was pretty handsome then and the girl was attractive. She was interested and very willing. I asked her to the movies." A half-smile burrowed into his cheek. "I was scared to death."

I forced a chuckle.

"I chickened out," he sighed. "I took her to Vienna, but at the entrance to the refugee camp, I told her to wait while I went up and got my money. I went in and said to the guys, 'No way am I going back out. You have to tell her to go away!'" He pressed his lips together and shook his head.

"A nice Catholic boy," I said, relaxing.

"I was still getting over being a religious Catholic and sex was sin," he said. "These guys, for them it was a joke."

The seriousness of his tone caught me off guard. "So, that's the reason you're glad you're Jewish? Because if you had been then, you would have gone to the movies with the girl?" I said, a little peeved.

"No, I mean—" He paused and collected his thoughts. "The Catholic attitude toward life is you take all the crap and the dessert comes later," he said. "It is false. And this intermediary, the priest, interprets things to you and you're not supposed to think for yourself. So different from the kallah study group at the temple we've been in for so many years now. Reading the texts and commentary together, questioning, thinking, arguing. It is so meaningful, so human." He stopped in front of the deli, noticing two Hasidic men in black hats and baggy black suits walking ahead of us. "No," he said standing straighter, "I'm much more comfortable with Judaism." He looked the men up and down. "Not *that* kind of Jew, of course," he said gesturing toward them. He opened the door to the sandwich shop. "After you, Mr. Szabo," he said, jauntily.

[28]

After several days, she was moved from the critical care unit to a semi-private room that overlooked Central Park. As I walked up to the new building from the bus one late afternoon, I reflected on the fact that she had never been in a hospital before. I could not recall so much as a cold. She was vigorous, strong, healthy. Recovery was simply a matter of time, I thought, no other possibility was imaginable. I arrived to find her dozing upright in bed, her eyes shut, her mouth half open. I watched for a minute, but her chest was still. I stiffened, but then she moved her right hand over the sheet beside her leg, unconsciously smoothing and straightening it. Someone had closed the shades and I opened them so she could take in the sunset. I touched her shoulder.

"Peter," she said, blinking, "how are you, dear?"

"You made it to Fifth Avenue. I'm impressed," I said. "Nice view."

A thin smile emerged from her lips.

"I brought a *Newsweek*," I said.

"*Newsweek*?" she said, sounding dimly aware that this was yet another thing she should have recognized but did not.

"You remember Monica Lewinsky and Bill Clinton?" I said with excitement as I pulled the magazine from my bag. She loved a good scandal, especially a lascivious one, and she hated Clinton. "Well, he's finally admitted it."

I hoped the news might stoke her passions, but her expression remained flat.

"Now," I said, trying to remain cheerful, "let's take a look."

I helped her on with her glasses. She stared down at the cover for a while, then she licked her right thumb and drew the pages across one by one. The glossy magazine slipped on the cotton bed cover, and she tried to steady it with her left hand. I caught it before it hit the floor, found the story, and placed it back on her thighs.

"Here, read this," I said, pointing to the text.

She read aloud, carving each word. "On Monday ... Clinton became the first president ... to testify before a ... federal criminal grand ... jury investigating ... his own behavior." She stopped, took a deep breath, and continued. "That night, before a Super Bowl-sized ... audience, he became the first to ... admit he'd been unfaithful to the First ... Lady." She paused and glanced at me, then returned to the article. "On Monday Clinton became ... the first president to testify before ... a federal criminal grand jury," she said, showing no sign of realizing that she had read the passage moments earlier. She stared at the photographs. After a few minutes, she tried to turn the page, stopped, sighed, then tried again. When she could not get hold of the paper, she did not seem frustrated, but rather repeated her efforts as a robot might, without memory or emotion.

I slid onto the bed beside her. "Here," I said, "with the dark glasses, that's Lewinsky, remember? And there he is with Chelsea." She nodded, and I could not tell if her over-serious expression reflected genuine engagement or an attempt to please me. I flipped the pages. "Here, this piece is about how he admitted it. See his tie? They said Lewinsky gave it to him as a present. He wore it the day she testified to the special prosecutor as a show of support for her. Oh, man!" I looked at her, expecting to find her outraged and delighted by the tawdry details, but she just listened passively, and to the degree she seemed to feel anything, it appeared to be melancholy. I read her the rest of the story, and when I reached the end of the piece, I closed the magazine. "Amazing," I said.

She gazed out at the park, decoupled from the room. Then she said, "I feel sorry for Clinton and Monica."

I was surprised by her empathy, but pleased at her connection. "You hate the guy, Granny," I said, chuckling. "Why do you feel sorry for them?"

She turned to me and nodded, then looked back out the window. There was another long silence. "Because they love each other," she said. I nearly laughed, thinking she was making a joke, but her tone was pure and heartfelt, and I suppressed the reaction.

We watched the orange sun slip behind the expanse of dark green treetops, and I wondered if perhaps I had been wrong about her, caricatured her politics, her worldview, too starkly. The human drama of man and woman had engaged her much more than the conservative-versus-liberal political battle. It struck me that where people stood on the issues did not matter to her as much as their struggle to love and be loved. After a while she said to the trees, "It is difficult to be the president. All the dirt comes out."

An aide arrived with her dinner, whipped spinach and whipped meat, soft foods on doctors' orders. She was not able to hold silverware very well, so the orderly fed her, one patient spoonful at a time. She received the food willingly, though she took a long time with each bite, moving it around in her mouth as if trying to link the flavor with something familiar. Halfway through, she closed her mouth to the spoon and shook her head at the insistent orderly like a petulant toddler, only eating more when she was offered the sweet, pudding-like dessert.

When she finished, she eased her head back against the pillow and napped. It was almost time to leave for home, but I lingered, reading a book while she rested. From time to time I folded the book on my lap and watched her. Her mouth was open and occasionally she snorted. Her cheeks seemed to have more color than the day before, and I felt lifted by how she had engaged with the Clinton story by the end. She is improving, I told myself.

An aide strode into the room with a wheelchair. "O.K., Miss Maria, time to go downstairs!" he shouted.

Granny jolted awake, confused.

"Downstairs," said the orderly through a thick Caribbean accent, holding up a form in his hand. "You're supposed to have a CAT scan now."

Granny looked at me, still not understanding.

"It's a test," I said to her. "A CAT scan. Remember? You did that before. I guess the doctor wants another one to see how you are doing."

She seemed afraid and I took her hand, rubbing her knuckles with my thumb. "It's all right, I'll go with you."

The three of us took the elevator to the basement, then traveled a maze of hallways to the CAT scan unit where the aide left us. I pulled up a seat next to my grandmother, and we waited without speaking, her eyes fixed on the wall across from us. Her face looked weathered and her nose seemed larger, the hook more pronounced. Long wisps of white hair fell back over her head, as if windblown. A blanket covered her lap.

"What did you do the last time you were here?" I said, trying to reconnect with her.

Her trance continued and it did not appear she had heard the question. Then she blurted out, "Vácz!"

I leaned toward her and tried again. "Granny, what did you do the last time you were down here for a CAT scan?"

"Vácz!" she repeated.

"Did you say 'What'?" I said.

"Vácz," she said, turning toward me, sounding a little annoyed. "V-a-c-z. It is a town in Hungary, just at the bend where the Danube turns south."

Maybe there was a hospital there or a spa, I thought, or some awful prison. Did she believe she was there, or was she just associating this place with that one? It was evening, and the windowless waiting area was deserted. I heard faint murmurs and a shrill laugh. From time to time unseen doors clicked open and banged closed.

"I came here forty or fifty years ago," she said, raising her eyes to mine expectantly.

"Yes," I said.

Then a technician emerged from the CAT lab and wheeled her inside.

When she came out, they told us we had to wait for an orderly to take her back to her room, and we resumed our silent stares at nothing.

"He was a high official," she said.

"Who was?"

"My father, he was a high official in the post office."

I nodded.

Her mind seemed to be careening through her past, glancing off random moments. I sensed a large, almost physical object in my chest, which I identified as hope, and I became aware of how my initial relief at having been able to understand her thoughts immediately after the stroke, even through her labored and distorted speech, had acted like a steroid on my sense of hope, bloating it until it obscured emotion and reason. The moment I gained this insight, the object began to dissipate, and I acknowledged that the damage to her was deep and probably not reversible.

It was cold in the basement, as if the entire hospital's worth of air conditioning had settled down there for the night. I shivered. An orderly appeared and we retraced the route back to Granny's room. The orderly lifted her into the bed and soon after she began to tap her fingers and shake her leg.

"Do you need some help?" I said.

From the hallway I heard the curtains squeak open. When I kissed her goodbye, she grasped my hand, her eyes clear and fixed on mine. "*Szervusz*, Peter," she said, slurring. "Thank you."

I descended to the large glass atrium and out into the warm night. I stopped on the front steps and inhaled the thick summer air. Then I wept.

[29]

Her possessions were passing away to relatives, to Eve, to the antiques buyer, to charity, to the trash, and I longed to pull something from the flow before it was lost, before she was lost, something that would keep her presence with me. What thing? The chairs I was promised were nearly forgotten. They had not come from Hungary, from family. The old documents and little photo album had ended up in the box my father was bringing with us. I had placed them there after glancing at Eve, who seemed not to notice, or to care. My mental hold on the photo album was complete. In my mind, I saw it on my bookshelf and had built around that image a defense of numerous arguments as to why I should have it. But even the photos did not sate my desire to take something of hers with me, a desire that grew more fevered as the day wore on. And then I saw clearly what I wanted. I sat down at the antique desk, touched the grain of the wood, and opened one of the small drawers. There was a tarnished old key inside and I picked it up and rubbed it. Through the window I watched the Russians standing in the front yard, sipping sodas from McDonald's and tossing crushed burger wrappers into the back of the truck. One of the Russians spoke to the others, mimicking different voices as if telling a joke. Shouts of laughter washed through the open door, then receded to dull chatter. I gazed about the disheveled living room. The sleeve of an old coat stuck straight up out of an overstuffed bag of clothes, grasping at the air. Eve walked over and pressed a handful of blouses, along with the sleeve, into the bag. My father sat down on a plastic folding chair in the middle of the room and ate his sandwich. Under the chair I noticed what at first appeared to be a hat or a sweater made out of some odd, shaggy material. I was about to get up and put it in the clothes bag when I realized it was one of her wigs flopped over a small stand. I closed my eyes and turned away, and when I opened them, I saw my aunt looking at me. Her lips parted, as if she was about to say something, but anxious, I spoke first. "Did you ever live here?" I asked her.

"No, he threw me out," she said.

"Who did?"

"Emery."

"From here?" I said.

"No, from the Bronx, one night after we arrived," she said, admiring a shawl she had found. "I turned the radio up loud and he gave me a whack across the face. Then he found a place for me. You remember, Dani?" she asked in an even, almost pleasant tone.

"No," he said through a mouthful of egg salad, shaking his head, but from the glaze in his eyes, it was not clear that he had heard her. He swallowed hard. "On the way here, on the plane to this country, I remember that we stopped in Shannon, Ireland, to refuel," he said, "and then we stopped somewhere in Canada that was freezing cold."

"Newfoundland," said Eve. "We almost crashed because there was a storm. It was a terror. I sat in the back vomiting, and Dani spent the flight in the cockpit talking with the pilots."

"We arrived the fifth of July at Idlewild. That's JFK now," said my father. "I remember coming out of the airplane and it was like stepping into a blast furnace." He stopped to wash down the last of his sandwich with a bottle of iced tea.

"Ugh, God, that heat," Eve said, rolling her eyes.

"We took a bus to Grand Central Station," my father continued. "Emery and our mother met us there and took us to our apartment by taxi. It was pouring rain, humid. I remember the taxi going through these bleak streets of the Bronx. When I was a kid, we thought the United States was paradise. And then you arrive. No green, just concrete and metal fences and the whirling wind stirring up discarded newspapers in the street."

He seemed tired, tired from two days of lifting and sorting and deciding, tired from the effort of remembering, from reliving. He had not yet responded to Eve's question about recalling Emery's blow, his immediate answer a detour. It struck me that his obfuscation was a sign of his pain, and I felt profound sympathy and affection toward him. Yet even so, I moved against the current of avoidance with which I had floated so often in the past.

"Where was the apartment?" I asked him.

"Tremont and Belmont," he said. "Tremont was the big street, like Andrassy utca in Budapest. I think it was 1899 Belmont Avenue. We were on the third floor. On the corner was a playground. It was a terrible neighborhood, very working class. They were building the Cross-Bronx Expressway nearby. Probably would be dangerous to go there now."

"Did you have your own room?"

"I don't remember. Probably."

"And Emery?" I said.

"Emery was there," he said, his eyes briefly meeting mine. "Turned out he had no income and no job. He couldn't keep a job because of his personality, and he had these epileptic attacks. He wanted me to get to work, and you, too." He gestured at Eve.

She nodded.

"I had as little to do with him as I could," he said, shaking his head and frowning. "Always tension in the house. I was still going through breaking my internal bonds with the Catholics. He was a big Jew and he jumped on me to be a Jew and to be a Mason like him." He wrinkled his nose. "He was a socialist on top of everything else. I considered him lower class."

He looked around for something to do and seemed about to get up. Then he relaxed and, staring at the floor, nodded.

"He scared me to death with his epileptic attacks," he said. "He would fall to the ground, shaking, and there would be foam coming out of his mouth. My mother would grab a handkerchief or a cloth napkin to stuff in his mouth so he wouldn't bite his tongue." Helplessness shone in his eyes. "And he ... there was...." He paused. "There was one time...." He said stopped again. "He came up behind my mother while she was washing the dishes and he wrapped his arms around her."

He took a deep breath, then exhaled.

"I was on the sofa in the living room, reading, and I could see in the kitchen," he said. "She struggled to turn around and he tried to kiss her. She pushed him away. He punched her, I don't know, on the arm, and shouted, 'You are my wife,' something like that. My mother was furious, berserk. 'I will never love you,' she said to him. 'You are scum.' And then he hit her again."

He winced, his face red.

"She covered herself, then she shoved him hard against the stove, ran to the bedroom and locked the door. I could see when she ran past me that her nose was bleeding."

Silence filled the room, dark and complete. I starred at the floor and studied the drab olive carpet, my eyes tracing the outlines of a worn patch, and I noticed how ragged the whole rug was. I sensed the gazes of my father and my aunt and lifted my eyes to theirs in turn. There was a softness in my father's eyes that was partly sad, partly apologetic, aware for a brief moment of how much he had shut off from himself, from us, all these years. I glanced at my aunt. She wore an expression that was at once self-satisfied, pained, and sympathetic. I looked back down at the rug. I heard the clatter of plates as Eve returned to packing the dinnerware.

My father rose and headed to the bathroom, patting me on the head as he passed.

I got up and walked outside. At my appearance, the Russians went into the apartment and returned a minute later with the last few items for the immigrants. Then I watched as they argued over how to load the truck. Furniture spilled into the street. The sun glared off the top of an end table, highlighting a web of cracks in the varnish. There were water stains on the rocking chair seat cushion, and the lamp shades were dusty and yellow. Rust dotted the metal band around the edge of the coffee table. Before the men arrived, before the sorting and discarding, the pieces of furniture had been integral, even iconic, parts of the landscape of my grandmother's apartment. Within that landscape, the pieces had a certain beauty. Out in the daylight, jumbled and uprooted from their environment, they looked like junk.

[30]

I returned to the hospital daily, hoping for change, suppressing disappointment.

"Granny," I said one evening as I clutched the gate on the side of her bed. Then again, louder, "Granny."

She opened her eyes and yawned. "What time is it?" she said quietly.

"Six-thirty," I said, "after dinner."

She stared straight ahead and I fidgeted with the bed control.

"Should I raise the back a little?" I said, pressing the button. The bed hummed as she was moved into a sitting position. Her face was a little thinner, and the shine and healthy red and orange tones of her skin were renewed. Her eyes were much less cloudy, more alert. She took a deep breath and exhaled. I watched the trees across the street as they swayed in a strong fall breeze.

"I do not want to die," she said, in a raspy near-whisper. Her eyelids were red and folded, and the lines at the edges of her eyes were deep and droopy. My first instincts were to laugh or to pretend I did not hear her. I forced myself to smile, but I could not look her in the eye.

"You're not going to die," I said as firmly as I could.

She turned her attention to the window. They had changed her room again, and instead of the park, she now looked out on a small grove of trees surrounded by pavement and buildings.

"We're on Madison Avenue now," I said. "The buildings there across the way are a housing project. And those are London plane trees. They are in a small playground."

I glanced at her for a sign that my description of her new location had grounded her, soothed her. Someone had placed a white knitted cardigan on her lap, and she folded and unfolded it with her right hand, the sound of her fingers against the textured garment rippling into the silence. She buttoned the buttons on the sweater, unbuttoned them, then started again. I noticed the pile of Impressionist postcards on the windowsill and went over to get them.

"Here," I said, sitting on the side of the bed and setting the cards on top of the sweater, "these are nice."

She flipped through the cards, studying each one with a long, empty stare. After a while she gazed up at me, a question in her eyes, wondering who had made these images, what they were. I thought the pictures would at least comfort her, even if she could not remember the artists, but the cold absence of recognition in her expression shook me. I will come every day, I swore to myself, I will teach her, as long as it takes. The mad flash washed over me, and I turned away from her as she continued to fumble through the postcards. I thought about how little she had changed, how little her mind had changed, over the past few weeks, even though the swelling around her brain must have subsided.

"Boring," she said, putting the cards down, and I turned back to her, startled. "You must be bored."

"No, Granny," I said, stroking her forearm, "I like coming to see you and just visiting."

"You will go and tell Norah how boring it was," she said plaintively, but in addition to her familiar dramatic manner, there was something girlish in her voice, faint notes of flirtatiousness.

"No, no," I said. "I'm glad I'm here."

"Thank you, dear Peter. Thank you for coming."

"My dad is coming tomorrow. He'll be staying with us," I said, starting to pack my things. "I am busy with this work project, but I'll come by, probably in the middle of the day."

She watched me close up my backpack and put on my jacket. "Thank you, dear Peter," she said. "You are a great grandson."

I zipped up my coat, returned to the bedside and held her hand. "And you are a wonderful grandmother," I said, chuckling.

"I try," she said shyly.

We held hands for a minute, and I looked at her as she gazed down at the sweater.

"You mean a lot to all of us," I said. "To me."

The stronger side of her face was turned toward me and I watched the smile spread from her mouth, to her cheeks, to her eyes. She moved her hand so that it was flat against mine and we patted our palms together lightly. "You are my best friend," she said.

"Should I put these in the garbage cans?" I asked Eve, gesturing to a number of bulging green plastic bags in the living room.

"Yes, next to the cans, they are full," she said.

I made a half-dozen trips to the trash, then stood in the doorway, out of breath and frustrated at the disarray that still ruled the room. "What are we going to do with all this stuff?" I asked my father, an edge in my voice. I felt vaguely angry and could not understand why he did not take control, why he did not put things in order.

"I don't know," he said, looking perplexed, and I sensed he was wondering why it was not I who was taking care of things, taking care of him.

"All those bags, they will go to the other charity," Eve said with authority. "The super said he will take care of it tomorrow. Did you give him some money, Dani?"

"No, I told him he could have the table," said my father, only half paying attention to her.

"The dining table?" said Eve. Her shoulders raised as if she were preparing to pounce on him. Her body became less rigid, though her eyes narrowed. "Dani, I'm giving the carpet to Janet, okay? You know, the one she made?"

He nodded without looking at her and then reached for an old photo high up on the wall.

"And there was some more jewelry," she said, holding the back of a dining chair and leaning forward, her tone honeyed, yet controlled. "I thought I would hold it for us for now."

He searched some piles of paper for the list of possessions that were to be kept and distributed among the family, found it, and began writing. Eve walked around the table, picked up a roll of packing tape, and began to seal up the china box. Her gentle expression was gone, replaced by deep lines of annoyance around her eyes and mouth. "You know," she said, stretching a long piece of tape across the box, "I want to say something from earlier."

I had started toward the back room but paused before entering the hallway, snagged by the slight sharpness of her tone.

"Emery she grew up with, but she didn't think," she said, tapping her temple with her index finger. "Me, a child who grew up totally sheltered, I saw Emery and I knew this is a match made in hell." She thrust out her lower lip. "She either didn't know, or she did and she went ahead anyway."

She seemed to be waiting for us to challenge her, even to want us to do so. I risked a glance at my father. He appeared immersed in the task of stacking framed photos in a box, but then he set one down and rested his hands on the side of the box.

"I don't know why he took to this violence," he said, incredulous. "His family wasn't like that at all."

It was as if he had never tried to think it through before, as if the events had been buried immediately after they had happened, buried deeply so as to prevent reflection. He looked at me, wanting an explanation. But I just stood there, mute and numb.

"He was a very troubled man," he said, anger beginning to replace confusion. "He hated blacks, and because of his epileptic problems and personality, he didn't hold a job very long. Always insisted everything was half. My mother pays half, he pays half. Often he wasn't working, so she had to pay her half, his half, everything."

Eve seemed a little pleased he had taken up the argument. "I don't want to sound like I'm criticizing," she said, "but she and our father fought, too, you remember?"

"He never hit her," my father said.

But she parried the point. "Yes, and it could have been a lot Father's fault, the arguments. He had high blood pressure. He was an excitable person. Who am I to say?" She paused. "But listen, there was a judge who did marital cases on Long Island and was famous enough to get a radio program. He said he never met a couple where it was always one person's fault only." Her body tilted forward as if physically taking the offensive. "So you can't blame Emery only. In his naïveté he expected a ready-made family who was going to love him."

"I never liked him," said my father to me as he sat down on the sofa, "from the first moment."

"Family, love, my mother had no such designs," said Eve, ignoring my father. "She used him."

"She wanted to get out of Hungary," I said. "To get you out."

"Absolutely," she said, "and I'm grateful to her. But you have to understand, he loved her since he was a teenager. Finally he can get her and she hates him. He was devastated."

"Why didn't she leave him?" I said. I didn't want to see things from Emery's perspective.

"Oh, she left many times," Eve said. "But he always tracked her down."

My father nodded. "Usually he kept calling her or waited for her at her work, asking her to come back," he said.

"And for a price, a fur coat or a diamond ring, she always went back," said Eve. "Emery's sisters and Alex, they paid her off."

I had wondered about her few items of luxury. They had seemed a stretch for a government paycheck.

"I mean really leave him," I said, recalling the story my grandmother had once told me about her time on the Upper West Side. "For good."

"Well, there was one time she was gone for weeks," said my father. "She went to some kind of hotel in Manhattan."

"The Paris," I said.

"I don't know," he said. "I cried and I begged her. She wouldn't have come back otherwise."

"She could have opened a fabric store or a dressmaking shop," I said hopefully. "She had a store in the fancy part of Budapest. She could make dresses with her eyes closed."

I wanted to believe that she would not compromise principle for anything. I wished that she had set out on her own and succeeded.

"No," said Eve. "To be a store owner in America is a different ballgame than in Hungary. I don't mean to take anything away, but in Hungary Oscar helped her, loaned her money. Here that was not possible."

"But—" I said.

She held up her hand. "Peter, I tell you, I go to the supermarket, and I'm not whining — well, maybe a little whining," she giggled, then grew serious again. "I go to the supermarket, I look like a duck, I walk like a duck, I dress like a duck, until I open my mouth. I can't tell you how many times this happened. I'm a friendly person. Somebody would start to talk to me. I would start to talk. They hear the accent and that's the end, because they equate accents with ignorance."

On the sideboard in the dining room was a black and white photograph of my grandmother at midlife. I glanced at it. A wide smile lit her face, something high over the photographer's shoulder seemed to hold her attention.

"So I would say, 'Now listen, let's stop for a minute. I can do this in four languages. Would you like to start over?'" Eve's eyes were wide and her cheeks raised. "See, if I talk to you and I sound intelligent, don't treat me like I'm a lousy immigrant. Europeans are better educated than Americans. I know Russians come here very, very well educated. They have a thick accent, but that doesn't mean they're stupid," she said. "As different as we were, I can imagine how my mother felt."

"The hurdle, too high," I said.

"Look at me," she said, lowering her voice. "I will not open my mouth in a supermarket because of that, so can you imagine what she must have felt? It must have been horrible, very painful. She never caught her footing here."

I gazed at my great uncle's painting of the Margaret Island gardens, my eyes settling on my grandmother, seated on a bench under a weeping cherry tree. I felt hatred toward Eve for her relentless opinions, for her directness, for the tint of truth that colored the story she sketched of my grandmother struggling against impossible barriers of language and money. I hated her for forcing me to let go of childish caricature and face the ambiguities, the nuances of adult life. I heard my father grunting. He was on his hands and knees, straining to reach the cable hookup behind the TV. I thought about helping, but a metallic rolling noise out on the street distracted me, followed by a slam. I went to the window and watched the Russians lock up the rear door of the truck. An instant later, the truck growled to life and lumbered down the street.

"I have this fantasy," I said, still staring out the window, speaking as if to myself, yet loud enough for my father to hear, "that at some point, after she went to work for the City, she and Emery reached a sort of truce, that it was peaceful, if not pleasant." As my voice gained pitch, I understood that this was more a question than a statement.

My father grunted again. "Maybe," he exhaled, his hips wiggling with effort.

"I just wish —" I started, then feeling defeated, I stopped. "I guess she had no one to turn to, nowhere to go."

He emerged from the back of the TV and placed his hands on his thighs. "Well, excuse me," he said, his face red, his voice rising. "She had her daughter, who was a basket case, and she had her son, who was living in comfort and peace in Washington and who didn't lift a finger."

He stared at the TV for a few moments.

"I don't know if she ever raised the question, whether she would like to come live with us," he said, wondering aloud. "But all her friends were up there. Later, her brother Pauli was in Washington. But that was just Pauli. Her natural place was New York." He nodded, as he took a seat, then he exhaled, and his shoulders melted. "Once she became ill, she still should have come down." He stared at the carpet.

"It must have been difficult living with him," I said.

He looked at me.

"Emery," I said. "Living with him must have been difficult for you, too."

He glanced at his uncle's painting of sunflowers.

"It was awful." He paused. "I never felt." He stopped and considered the ceiling. "Maybe during some of those air raids." He paused again, struggling to express himself, determined to try. "But you see," he said, our eyes meeting, "the war was to me some kind of adventure. I didn't get hurt, though bombs fell everywhere. You could see the ruins, the destruction, but I was not scared." He nodded. "The first time that I was afraid in my life was in that apartment," he said, "because of Emery and what he might do out of anger."

He gathered up the TV power cord and snapped a rubber band on it. He picked up a stack of papers, placed them in a box, and folded it closed. I passed him some packing tape. He sealed the box and started to slide it over to the door. I scanned the room purposefully, as if searching for something to do. Then he stopped and stood up, a spasm of anger rising from his chest. His whole body grew taut, and for an instant he looked much younger. Surging currents of sadness seemed to swirl in his eyes, while hate threw a shadow across his face.

"When I was drafted into the army just after Korea, I was scared," he said, "but it was a relief to get away from that apartment. A relief."

He removed his glasses and rubbed his eyes. His cheeks sagged and the flesh hung loosely below his chin.

"I hated to leave her in the lurch," he said.

Then he looked at me stone-eyed.

"It was an escape," he spat. "I left her at this guy's mercy."

[32]

I stopped in the doorway. Her bed was freshly made and the area around it empty of vases, cards, and newspapers. Drawn shades blocked out what remained of the daylight. I hurried to the nurses' station. There I learned that she had been moved to the rehabilitation unit to start physical therapy. I turned the possibilities over in my mind as I tried to follow the nurse's directions to her new room. Left turn, then right, or was it left again? I kept on. Behind me the slow-paced rap of hard soles on linoleum echoed like rhythmic blows of an axe at the base of a tree. I heard the squeaky scratch of a bed screen, and it reminded me of the scraping of an old metal rake against the ground. I imagined myself lying on my bed, back home, in childhood, as the rake scraped again and again outside my open window. A cool breeze filtered through the shutters next to my head, and I rolled over and checked the clock. 7:30 a.m. She was already up and out. I opened one shutter a crack and watched her as she pulled the rake toward her in stiff, sure motions, moving back and forth along a line of leaves, building them up like a wave. She stopped to rest, her cheeks flushed, a slight smile on her face, the back lawn now three-quarters clear of the signs of fall. Later that afternoon, I took a break from playing Nerf basketball in my room and headed to the kitchen for a glass of water. A flash of sunlight caught my eye and through the dining room curtains I found its source out on the patio. My grandmother was sitting in a chair with her face pointed toward the sun and her eyes closed. In her lap she held a three-paneled reflecting board about the size of a large Chinese restaurant menu. She adjusted the panel so that it gathered still more of the sun and the intense light splashed her face and sprayed golden streaks of varying width across her chest. There was an easiness to her posture that suggested profound relaxation. For an instant, she appeared to float.

A beeping monitor drew me back to the hospital hallway and doubt as to whether I had made the last right turn I was supposed to make. Then from somewhere nearby, I heard my father's voice, and I followed it until I found him standing in a hallway with Eve and my mother. The three of them stopped talking as they saw me. I smiled, yet it did not change the intense expressions on their faces. They seemed to be making up their minds about something. My father broke the awkward silence.

"She hasn't spoken all day," he said.

"She just looks around the room," said Eve. "She looks at you for a minute if you ask her something, then she stares around the room again."

We all avoided eye contact.

"They found a bladder infection," my father said, in the flat and formal tone of a news anchor. "They inserted a catheter to relieve her. She will need it regularly." He paused, then he added, "For a while."

His saying this to me appeared to be a kind of release for the three of them, as their expressions softened. But I felt anxious.

"Can you imagine?" Eve said. "A woman of her sensibilities? A catheter?"

Around dinnertime, a young woman cradling a clipboard poked her head into the room and motioned us outside. "You remember the test I gave her earlier?" she said to my father. "We call it a swallow test because it tells us whether, or how much, her incident has affected her ability to manage food and liquid."

She looked at the rest of us for the first time.

"Well," she said, as she tapped the clipboard with a pen, "she failed."

She rocked forward and back several times from her heels to the balls of her feet. We passed confused glances to one another.

"She's aspirating," the woman explained, "which means that much of the food she has eaten over the last week went down the wrong pathway. There is some danger of pneumonia."

Though her eyes were narrow and serious, she seemed pleased with her correct diagnosis, judging from the incongruous curve of satisfaction that had forced its way to the corners of her mouth. I started to ask a question, but at that moment the staff doctor joined the circle. He was a tall bald man in his mid-thirties, with a round face and a kind expression.

"So you've gotten the news?" he said.

We nodded like obedient schoolchildren.

"This is a complex situation, but there are a couple of options. Feeding tube down the throat," he said to me and my mother, then, turning toward my father and Eve, "or a peg." Sensing we did not understand this, he added, "A peg, that's where we put something like a spigot in her side and run a tube into her stomach." He poked the paunch above his hip. "We pump a nutrient solution through it."

I stared at his belly, then back at his face.

"I recommend the peg," he said. And though he spoke with cool authority, he seemed also to reach out to us through the rounded corners of his eyes, trying to soothe us. "She will be much more comfortable with a peg than with the throat tube, and she will be better able to concentrate on learning to swallow."

"That's right," the woman said, as if on cue. "Many people can be taught how to swallow food again. She's a good candidate and we can start tonight, whatever you decide about the peg. Or the throat tube."

I felt dazed, and I could tell from their slouches that the others did, too. I asked the therapist how re-learning how to swallow food worked.

"Oh, well, it's a little complicated," she said, clutching the clipboard to her chest. "But, sort of simply, you hold the food on one side of your mouth with your tongue, take a breath, hold the breath, then kind of push the food to the back of your throat." She ran her fingers down her neck.

"But how," I said, "how does—" then I stopped.

The doctor touched my arm. "I can imagine how many questions you all must have, how you must be feeling right now," he said. "Unfortunately, with the risk of pneumonia, we need to move fairly quickly. Why don't we leave you for a bit?" He checked his watch. "I'll be back in a half-hour or so."

We talked it through, but there seemed to be no choice really. As we spoke, a stinging cold enveloped me, and I felt frozen in place.

Granny awoke but said little. From my bag I pulled a letter my sister had asked me to give to her.

"Nancy?" she said, straining to sit up a little more in her bed, recognition crossing her face. She took the letter with her strong hand and brought it up to her eyes. She spent a minute studying it, confused at first, as if she had expected to see a photograph of my sister, rather than a page full of words. Her eyes moved around the sheet of paper, then she spoke. "Dear Granny," she said. She had been quiet for so long that the familiar, if altered, sound of her voice brought the immediate and startled attention of the others, who had been chatting at the end of the bed.

"I am writing to you from the Netherlands," she continued. One side of her mouth seemed limp and lifeless, while the other labored over the sounds as if they were heavy objects hauled with great effort from her mind to her lips, where they were forced out with equal exertion. I leaned over and placed my finger at the start of the next sentence.

"It is Steve's sabbatical year and we are spending it here," she said, exhaling, then taking a deep breath. "Benjamin and I have started to," she stopped, waiting for me to move my finger to the next line, "explore the parks and the nearby towns."

She read on, working her way through the words as if climbing a long, steep staircase, pausing from time to time. After a page and a half, she stopped and set the letter down. She stared at it, distracted. Our eyes were wide, and we urged her on wordlessly. She looked around but did not seem to see us. Then she lifted the paper and began to read aloud again. After a few seconds we realized she was starting from the top of the page, re-reading a paragraph she had just finished without realizing it. There was a slight hollowness in her voice, and she seemed to concentrate completely on shaping the sounds of the words, their meaning glancing off her mind. Though the letter continued, when she reached the bottom of the page, she laid it at her side and did not pick it up again.

[33]

The physical therapy room resembled a miniature health club. To the left of the doorway ran a row of strengthening machines, and to the right, along one wall, was a line of padded benches. Across the room, a therapist lay sprawled on a large blue mat, demonstrating a stretch for a middle-aged man. A pink scar curved across the back of the man's shaved head. The therapist moved through a series of contortions like a yoga master, explaining each move in bright chatter as the man watched her.

Because Granny had not been on her feet since the stroke, I did not notice her standing in the middle of the room. Then my eyes found her and I felt a jolt of hope. She wore a pale blue hospital gown and slippers, and she clenched a walker with white, knobby knuckles. Her head hung down like a streetlight. Her therapist, a taut, mid-twenties blonde in spandex and a doctor's coat, whisked around Granny on a rolling stool, speaking at a high-yet-friendly volume. "Maria, one step at a time now," she said, staring at Granny's feet as if she had just issued them an order. After a second's hesitation, Granny's left leg slid forward, as if it were a self-conscious young soldier. "Good!" said the therapist. "Your head now, lift it." There was no response to the command. "Look at me, Maria," said the therapist, cheerfully, yet forcefully. "Look at me!"

Granny obliged, straightening her upper back, then raising her head with a series of small, deliberate jerks. Our eyes met, and she squeezed the right side of her face into what looked like a smirk. The therapist wheeled around.

"That's the first time she's smiled all day!" she said, "And I've tried all of my jokes!"

I introduced myself.

"It's great when family comes," she said warmly. Her red-orange cheeks and shiny eyes glowed with energy, and I was certain she could pour a little of herself into Granny and repair her.

"Who's that, Maria?" she said, pointing to me.

Granny bounced her head slightly, still staring at me. "Peter."

"Yes, that's right! Now walk over toward him."

She lowered her head and gazed at her feet, then started to shuffle in my direction, first the right foot, then the left, like a child learning to ice-skate.

"Good!" said the therapist, turning and smiling at me. "She took only five steps yesterday. That's fifteen today!"

This was enormous progress to the young woman, yet I could not help but think about the walk from the National Gallery to the White House, which Granny had done not too many weeks earlier. How many steps had that been? I watched Granny as she continued to shuffle. Her face, though still somewhat puffy, seemed shinier than in the previous few days, and the exertion of the therapy had brought color to her cheeks. I wondered whether she was thinking about the irony of re-learning walking. As she reached me, she offered a thin smile and paused, waiting for a response from me. I felt bitter and twitched awkwardly, then something warm spread through my mind. I touched her hand. "Wow, Granny, that was great," I said.

The therapist helped her into a wheelchair and knelt down in front of her. I sat on one of the padded benches next to them. "Let's start to work on standing up," said the therapist, moving Granny's good right hand to the arm of the wheelchair. "Now, lean forward and press up with your legs, hard as you can."

Granny rose gradually, trembling with effort, stood, then curled back into the wheelchair.

"All right!" said the therapist. "Another one!"

Granny stood once more, after a great struggle, but could not manage a third try.

The therapist stroked Granny's thigh.

"Maria, you may be tired, you've done so much today," she said earnestly. "Do you think you can work on one last thing?"

Granny's eyes drooped, but she nodded and the therapist helped her to the bench next to me, then knelt in front of her again. Granny began to list toward me, and the therapist and I both moved to shore her up.

"Yes, this is what I want to talk about with you," she said, gripping Granny's shoulder and holding her upright. "This is a sitting exercise," the therapist said. "Because of the stroke, your left side is much weaker than your right." She patted one shoulder, then the other as she spoke. "Some of it may not even feel that good. This affects your sense of balance and makes it hard to keep from falling over. Do you understand me?"

Granny raised her chin, then lowered it.

The therapist's gaze intensified as she studied Granny's face. Her eyes narrowed and her smile flattened as a look of hard determination replaced airy encouragement.

"You have to overcompensate for your tendency to fall to the left by leaning to the right," she said. "Got it?"

Granny grunted.

The therapist let go. "Lean to the right, Maria. Think, 'I must lean to the right.'"

Granny sat motionless for several seconds, then she started to sag to the left. The therapist caught her and pressed her back into place. "Good!" she said through a broad smile. "Let's try again."

[34]

I slid the hall closet doors back and forth. Empty. I poked my head in the bathroom, then scanned the back room before returning to the living room. "The back is pretty much clear," I said. "Looks like we're almost done."

"Almost," said Eve, heavily. "So many little things still, and no one has finished with the kitchen. Dani, did you finish with the kitchen?"

There was not much left to sort through, but my father and Eve were worn out and I was unsure whether they would be able to resolve where the remaining possessions would go. I looked at the wig, still sitting on a small stand under a chair in the middle of the nearly bear living room. I felt empty, repulsed, then I leaned down and picked it up. "What about the wig?" I said.

Eve was standing in front of two paintings that hung in the dining room, studying them. I had not noticed them before. The wood frames were chipped, but ornate. The dark colors and the realism with which the scenes had been composed suggested the paintings might be old. I saw an expression cross Eve's face, like that of a child caught licking a cookie-batter bowl. "You know, we could get a lot of money for these, maybe tens of thousands."

I started to estimate how much might go to the grandchildren, then I stopped myself. Just another of her groundless assertions, I thought. Though as I looked again at the paintings, now with the sort of respect one confers on objects that may well have a great deal of value, it occurred to me that Eve might have shown them to the antiques dealer. Something brushed against my jeans and I looked down at the wig. I shook it at Eve.

"What about this?"

She took the wig. "I don't know," she said. "Poor Granny." She dropped it into a large giveaway bag. "They are expensive, maybe someone can use it."

"And the Pauli paintings?" I said, scanning the sunflowers and the Margaret Island scene.

"Maybe we will take the Margaret Island picture," my father said without looking up from the box he was taping.

"Have them both," Eve said.

Her indifference had an undertone of calculation, and I suspected she was keeping track and already had something in mind she would appropriate in return for having given my father their uncle's paintings. My eyes moved to the antique desk, then I studied Eve, who was wrapping china in the dining room. Her desires centered less on sentimental items than on things with monetary value. I wondered how much the antiques dealer had told her he would give her for the desk, and I knew the time was not long before a decision about it would be made. I picked up two bags and started for the door.

"That one is for charity," Eve said, waving a finger at me. "Leave it in the entry way, dear Peter, won't you?"

I dropped the giveaway bag at the doormat and brought the other one outside, where my father was trying to snap shut the lid of an overfull trash can. I started to speak, then paused. Part of me acknowledged that my grandmother was gone, even if she was still alive. And yet, another part of me held fast to memories and had a primal desire to possess something of hers that might embody her presence. Unspoken sensitivities and base motives were involved, and so over the last day and a half, the division of her belongings, the struggle for them, had been elliptical. I worried about crossing Eve's appetite for money, but I knew that with the desk I could not just wait and hope for generosity.

"Dad," I said, "what's going to happen to the desk?"

"The desk? Oh, I don't know. Eve has this antiques dealer," he said.

The dazed expression left his face as he comprehended my desire. It struck me that he had sought few items of hers. Perhaps this was a measure of his grief, reminders being painful to own. Yet there was also a characteristic selflessness about it, deep and sad, and also inspiring.

"You interested?" he asked.

I nodded.

"It's pretty wobbly," he said.

I shrugged. He smiled at me and I felt reassured.

"So we're almost done," he said.

"It's pretty much empty. Except the kitchen."

"Oh, yes," he said, returning to the task.

Needing a break, I sat down in the dining room and tried to think of something to say as I watched Eve wrap china and place it in a box with her name on it. "Did you go back to Hungary much?" I asked eventually.

"Yes, many years," she said. "Usually alone. Sometimes with Granny."

I gazed at a bright gold square of carpet in the living room on which a large chair had sat until a few hours ago. At the edge of the square the rug faded to a grayish brown and I noticed several large dust balls along the wall.

"What was it like?" I said.

"The first time was in '65. Ed came," she said, referring to her husband. "A lot of people who went back were arrested, you know, and they set all kinds of traps for us." She lowered her voice. "For instance, you couldn't change money, and many people approached your uncle Ed for dollars. But we talked about that before we left, that death was better than falling into a trap. So we didn't do that. Even at the Gellert Hotel, in the baths, they approached us to change money."

I had been staring at the stained and yellowed shade on the remaining floor lamp only half-listening, but the sound of a cupboard door slamming shut refocused me on Eve, who had sat down next to me.

"In the Gellert we saw my aunts Jancsi and Bözsi, and cousin Eva. It was wonderful. I wore a red coat and a red dress and everybody in Hungary wore gray. Terrible." She chuckled and tapped my knee.

"My aunt had lived in such opulence, and now the paint was cracked and everybody had only one room under the Communists. Bözsi *néni* took a bathroom and divided it into a kitchen, too. They looked so poor, it was horrible," she said, frowning. "You come back here and you want to kiss the ground."

My father came out of the kitchen with still more pots. "No one wants these, right?" he said. "We'll give them away."

"The last time I went was in 1988 for my class reunion," Eve said, after giving him a shrug. "You know, Peter, I am not a wealthy person. I have different kinds of riches." She touched her chest. "I took my white pleated skirt, an over-sweater, and white shoes, and I went to this reunion." She waved her hand in a circle. "It was in a plain restaurant with everybody around a horseshoe table. They were all fat and old, these poor girls and my old teacher, because they lived through communism. I told my best girlfriend not to tell anybody who I am."

The images emerged in my mind, the restaurant, the people, Eve in white. What was she? An angel? A bride? A ghost?

"Your old teacher?" I said. "That must have been special."

"I hated her, and she didn't like me either," she said, scowling. "Anyway, there was this star in the class who always sat proper and had long legs and high heels. We wore uniforms back then, but she was very mature, if you know what I mean. I was a simple, sheltered girl." she said.

"The star, she was sitting with the teacher, and she comes over to me and says, 'Tell me who you are.'" Her cheeks were full now with a wide, almost sinister smile. "And I say, 'No, you have to guess.' And, you know, she couldn't. So I told her." The percussive clatter of handfuls of silverware being dropped into a box echoed her laughter.

"I tell you, Peter, a good life is the best revenge," she said. "She says to me, this star girl, 'Who would have thought that the ugly duckling would become the swan?'" she said, still shaking with laughter. Then the smile left her face. "You see, freedom, it does something. Ugly or not ugly, rich or poor, there's something that affects you by living free. It is the way you walk, it is everything." She was pointing at me. "Maybe my mother knew what communism really was going to be, maybe not. Either way, she saved us."

[35]

It was late September and the air had changed. I wore a light sweater and a jacket. The sun surrendered a greater portion of each day to darkness. I nudged Granny and she awoke. "*Szervusz*, Peter," she said, glancing sideways as she tried to sit up a little straighter.

"How are you feeling?" I asked.

She just stared at the wall across the room.

"Did you have physical therapy today?"

"No, not today." She pinched her eyebrows into a frown. "Is Eve here?"

I put a hand on the sidebar of the bed. "No," I said, "she is coming to see you tomorrow."

"Oh," she said, still not looking at me.

I sat on the bed near her feet and looked out the window. The setting sun turned the brown bricks of the westward-facing buildings across the avenue orange.

"So, Norah and I are going away this weekend," I said, turning toward her.

"Where?"

"Up to northwestern Connecticut."

"Oh, that's nice," she said without interest.

"It's one of our favorite places," I said, injecting a forced brightness into my voice. "I'm hoping that the leaves have begun to turn."

She tapped the covers with her fingers.

"Tonight I'm meeting a friend for dinner. His mother is Hungarian." I waited for the spark this information was sure to produce.

"Oh?" she said.

I watched her hand, which was still patting the bed. "Granny," I said quietly, "you need help with something, right?"

She gazed down at her lap and nodded.

I went down the hall to find a nurse, past patients already asleep, past shade-darkened rooms haunted by low television murmurs and the irregular strobe of changing scenes. At the nurses' station, several nurses gossiped behind the counter, while another chatted with the shift doctor. I stood there, not wanting to interrupt, and studied a large whiteboard with the day's physical therapy schedule. Check marks next to Granny's name indicated completed sessions at eleven and three o'clock. I turned back to the nurses and watched them a bit longer, until one of them noticed me and lifted her eyebrows.

"It's my grandmother," I said in a low voice. "She's in 501A. She has Depends and needs some help." The nurse checked a list in front of her and told me someone would be right down.

"Where is Eve? Is Eve here?" Granny asked as we waited for the aide to come and change her.

"No, Eve is coming tomorrow," I said.

We sat for a while, then she said, "Do you speak Hungarian?"

"No," I answered.

"Not a word?" she said in total disbelief. "It is a lovely language. It is a shame you do not know a word. Eve, she speaks the most beautiful Hungarian," she said, singing each syllable of the word "beautiful." She straightened the covers. Eve had cut Granny's hair the day before and this had the effect of accentuating and simplifying her face, now dominated by gray eyes peering out through sagging flesh. She seemed to be neither woman nor man.

"Do you speak Hungarian?" she said again, breaking the silence.

"No," I said, shifting in my chair.

"Not a word?" she said, aghast, as if I had just told her about a hideous crime I had committed.

"No, my father never taught me."

An orderly slid into the room and drew the curtains around the bed. I fidgeted outside the door until he left.

"Do you speak Hungarian?" she asked again.

In the weeks since the stroke, I had tried to maintain our connection and to bolster her by adapting to each shift in her condition and meeting her where she was. Yet, though I strained to listen, to see into her, to interpret — and often succeeded — there were limits to how much I could comprehend.

"No," I said. "My father didn't speak Hungarian to us when we were growing up." I narrowed my eyes, not understanding where she was trying to go.

"He is a nasty father," she said, in the way a little girl might tell a parent how she felt about an evil storybook character.

I found her melodramatic critique of the son she worshipped, but now spoke of as if he were a stranger, both surprising and, in a way, humorous.

"No, he is a great father," I said, chuckling. "He just didn't teach me Hungarian."

Her determined pout did not weaken.

"All right," I said, as if engaging a child in a game, "what words should I know?"

"It is a beautiful language," she said earnestly, "and so easy to learn."

I was about to point out the extreme difficulty of the language, but I was glad for her eagerness and instead asked, "How do you say, 'I'll see you later?'"

"*Később látlak,*" she said, pronouncing it loudly and slowly. Since the stroke, the left side of her mouth had lagged behind the right, causing a slur in her voice, yet as she spoke these words in her native tongue, the sounds were crisp.

I pulled a small notebook and a pen from my backpack and repeated the words as I tried to write them down. "Keesup laytuk."

"*Nem,*" she said, shaking her head. She said it phonetically. "Keeshub," she said pausing.

"Keeshub," I repeated.

She nodded. "Lah-tek."

"Lah-tek."

She smiled.

"What other words should I know?" I said.

After a few moments she drew a breath and looked at me. "*Szeretlek,*" she said. "I love you." She gazed at her lap. Then she sounded it out for me, "Seh-reht-lek. The most important words."

"Seh-rhet-lek," I said. "*Szeretlek.*"

She nodded and her face lightened. "*Nagyon.* Very much," she said. "*Nagyon szeretlek.* I love you very much."

"Naj-your ser...."

"Na-j-yo," she interrupted. "Yo," she said, dropping her jaw and forming the "o" as best she could. "Yo."

"Naj-yo *szeretlek,*" I said.

"Naj-yo," she echoed, trying to perfect my pronunciation, her mouth still holding the "o" after she finished speaking.

"Naj-yo," I said. "How do you spell it?"

She gestured for my small pad and pen, then with her good hand she wrote each letter in an unsteady script that ran diagonally across the page. The handwriting was nearly as elegant as it had once been. As her hand reached the edge of the page, the letters began to compress, then curl up along the spiral binding. "Nah," she grumbled as she turned the pen over and began to rub it back and forth across the ink.

"It's a pen, Granny," I said, and she looked up at me as if I had disturbed her from a daydream. "It won't erase." I took the book from her and turned the page. "You can do it again on a fresh sheet if you like."

She wrote it a second time, neater and straighter, setting the pen down when she finished. "The most important words," she said.

We looked at one another in silence, her eyes so bright and clear I could not look away. In them, I recognized a delight and affection I had seen in the past when I had brought her a moment of intense joy. At the same time, I became aware of something cracked and broken in those eyes and felt the mighty tide of sadness within her, as if, briefly, she had opened to me her limitless grief.

"Never forget the words," she said. "Be careful with them."

My eyes filled and I turned away and gathered my things. "Granny, I am late for dinner," I said. I slung my backpack over my shoulders and took hold of her hand. "*Később látlak*," I said, smiling. "Was that good?"

She chuckled. "Yes," she said.

"*Nagyon szeretlek*," I said, tightening my grip.

"*Nagyon szeretlek*," she said, letting go.

[36]

My father closed several kitchen drawers with a series of bangs. "Say, Eve," he said as he appeared in the doorway, "I don't think I will have room in the car on the way home for the old paintings. How about if we store them at Peter's for now? I was going to do the appraisal up here anyway, and he is right in the city."

The clever positioning surprised me. Perhaps he had been paying closer attention to her division of things than I had believed. Yet, while there was a certain aggression in his casual suggestion, I saw his intervention as being motivated less by avarice than by a desire to ensure a fair outcome. If the paintings had gone with her, they, or the cash they brought, might not be seen again.

"Yes," she said vaguely, a part of her still lingering at her reunion.

"And the desk, too," he said, nodding at it. "Peter's, until we decide."

I tried to look oblivious, reaching down to pick up some papers and stuff them in the trash.

She looked at him, then me, then the desk. Her attention had returned to the present and her eyes bore into the desk as if recalibrating its value. She started to say something, then she stopped. "Fine."

Excited and grateful, I got up and followed my father into the cramped kitchen. He finished dumping the contents of the refrigerator into a garbage bag, and I stacked an assortment of glasses, no two of which seemed to match, in a box, stopping to examine a glass embossed with faded palm trees.

"What's this?" my father said.

He stood in front of a large paper calendar pinned to the bulletin board on the wall by the doorway. The calendar displayed August, the torn remains of earlier months forming an uneven band at the top of the page. The days were labeled in a plain font and arrayed in a typical grid, week atop week. A series of X's, handwritten in thick blue marker in the day squares, formed a disturbing, lopsided design. Neat and symmetrical the first week, they began to vary in shape and size across the second, and by the middle of the third week, they were nearly illegible. Tuesday and Wednesday had been marked with little more than crossing squiggles. Thursday's X was large, with one elongated slash tailing off down into the following week.

I studied the writing. Reading the days backward, the marks brought to mind the progression of a child's penmanship as she learned to write, and I smiled and gazed back at the calendar. My eyes followed the marks forward in time until they ended at Friday, August 21st. That box contained only a short segment of a line, which started in the upper right-hand corner and moved to the center. Where it had been interrupted, there was no ink bleed and no trailing scribble. The line simply stopped. I imagined my grandmother lifting her hand from the page to touch her temple as her head grew light, a pool of black occluding her vision. Then I smothered the thought with an alternative picture. Wearing an apron that protected her pantsuit, she had started to draw the line, but then glanced at the clock. She was breaking the rule she had made for herself, a rule I had just invented, under which the dinner dishes had to be washed before marking the day accomplished. But this manic picture offered only a flimsy barrier.

My father exhaled through tight lips, removed the calendar, and stuffed it in one of our boxes. Then I picked up the box and carried it out to the car.

The cleanout exhausted me, but I drifted in and out of sleep. My father was staying over with us before returning home in the morning, and late that night I was roused by snoring in the living room. I listened. Deep inhale, stuttering snort, loud and breathy exhale, occasionally collapsing into a sigh. It sounded as if he were having a muffled conversation. I got up and went to the bathroom, and when I came out, there was silence. I sat down at the dining table and eyed his large belly for a sign of life. What he could not say with words he said with food, I thought, and I recalled a dinner from long ago, my father refilling his plate with potatoes, corn, and chicken. Was it for the third time? When he finished, he picked leftovers from my sister's plate, then mine. His physical hunger long sated, he ate mechanically, instinctively, a trance-like mask on his face. Attempts to reason with him about eating were met with defensiveness and rage. Over time, we developed the strategy of placing the serving dishes in whatever space was available as far from his reach as possible, assembling the food behind a sort of Maginot Line comprised of the sugar bowl, napkin holder, and salt and pepper shakers. This only triggered angry lectures about leaving food over when there were starving children in the world.

His belly moved up and down, like the gentle swell of the sea. In place of the anger that usually arose when the topic was my father's weight, I felt fresh understanding. Crowded with strange families in a dark cellar, the sounds of bombs overhead, first muffled and distant, then earsplitting, crashing, shaking. Would the building collapse? he must have feared. Would mother return? Fear without protection, without comfort. I had had no idea.

He snorted and rolled to his side. Perhaps he had been among the starving as he hid in that dark cellar on Üllői út, waiting for his mother and possibly food, I thought. The confusion must have made it worse — pulled from Jesuit school and told he was Jewish, a Yellow Star pinned to his chest, awakened during the night, marched down to the courtyard, people taken away. Had he had to drop his pajamas to prove he was not circumcised? False papers. A Catholic by upbringing, a Jew by blood and edict, pretending to be a Catholic. There without his mother, without a father. It made sense, his impulse to numb. Not an absence of feeling, but a suppression of feeling, a buffering of memory, of pain, and of anger as a final defense when this failed. Yes, it made sense.

I went to the futon and sat next to him as he slept, his hands folded under his cheek, his breathing more even. I felt something settle within me, and a sense of sympathy and affection grow. I patted his shoulder gently and watched over him for a time. Then I got up, went back to the bedroom, lay down, and listened to Norah's soft, steady breathing next to me. I touched her back and soon fell asleep.

A few weeks later I came across an ad for a lecture at the 92nd Street Y and decided to head over and see if there were still seats available. With ticket in hand and an hour or so to kill before the event, I drifted up to the library. Once inside, I paused. The part of me that wanted to know more about the historical context of my family's wartime experience in Budapest, to put the many story fragments together into some sort of whole, had long struggled against a strong, dark object that worked to suppress this desire. Recently, I had sensed the suppression ease. I approached the librarian and inquired about whether they had Randolph Braham's great work, *The Politics of Genocide: The Holocaust in Hungary*. As I had learned from the jacket of the massive bibliography I had purchased at West Side Judaica, Braham, a professor at the City University of New York, had survived the Holocaust in Hungary and had spent a lifetime chronicling its political and operational aspects in minute detail. In a minute I found myself searching a row of stacks in the back. It did not take long before my eyes caught his name on the binding of a three-inch-thick book, *The Politics of Genocide: The Holocaust in Hungary, Volume 1*. Its equal-sized companion stood next to it. I did not know when I would return there, or whether I might locate the book elsewhere, so since there was still time before the talk, I pulled down Volume 1, sat on a shelving stool, opened to the Preface, and started to read.

Sometime later, a chair screeched against the floor as someone got up to leave the library, which briefly shattered my concentration, before I returned to the passage I had just read.

> Uninformed, unprepared, and basically disunited, Hungarian Jewry consequently became easy prey for the SS and their Hungarian accomplices after the occupation. The Final Solution program—the isolation, expropriation, ghettoization, concentration, and deportation of the Jews—was carried out at lightning speed. In late spring 1944, close to 440,000 Jews from all over Hungary, excepting Budapest, were deported to Auschwitz within less than two months.

"Excepting Budapest." Something disturbed my stomach and my palms grew moist beneath the cellophane cover of the heavy work in my lap. "Excepting Budapest." The words again filled my mind. I flipped to the contents pages and checked my watch. I pulled Volume 2 from the shelf, purchased a copy card, and began photocopying the Budapest chapters. Sweat dampened my shirt as I rushed the dull, mechanical work, sensing glances from the librarian and the few others in the room. The stack of copies thickened in the tray of the moaning machine.

"Sam! Sam!" I heard a woman shout. I looked up from the binder. A young mother shook her head at a little boy who was staggering away from her, shrieking with delight. "Oh goodness. Come back here!" she said with a defeated sigh as she got up to corral her child, leaving the banal yet relaxing conversation she had been having with her friend, who herself sat beside a stroller that cradled a sleeping girl.

I sipped my tea and observed the midafternoon crowd that had filled Starbucks — mothers and strollers, a chattering group of middle-schoolers overflowing with near-summer energy, people tapping away on computers. I often went there to work when I needed a block of time for report writing or craved the presence of others. I had arrived late morning, having resolved to crack the Braham material, and had taken a corner table in front with a view of Broadway out the large windows. I had only reached late summer of 1944, but I was not sure how much more I could stand. It was difficult to think straight. Braham had told of Hungary's alliance with Germany, with which it shared certain cultural affinities, and, more important, a desire to reverse the putative treaties that ended the First World War, treaties that, among other things, reduced Hungary's territory by two-thirds. Hungary's engagement in the war was complex. The anti-Jewish crusade of the government was real and yet somehow faint-hearted. The double-talk the Hungarians offered the Germans, who pestered them for more aggressive action against the Jews, was almost humorous. The ability of the Hungarians to hold in mind two opposite views — vitriolic anti-Semitism and the quaint sense of honor toward fellow countrymen of a long-fading landed nobility — reminded me of my grandmother's hatred of Bill Clinton and her sympathy for his relationship with Monica Lewinsky. How utterly Hungarian she was.

With the Soviets having turned the tide of the war in the east, the Nazis no longer abided Hungary's delays. Hitler met with Hungary's ruler, Admiral Horthy, in early March of 1944 and concluded an agreement that facilitated German occupation of the country and removal of the Jews for "work in Germany." More euphemisms. More double-talk. Admiral Horthy, an old-school nobleman, found himself very much in the midst of a tightening bind with gruesome and extraordinarily dishonorable implications. Admiral Horthy. I thought of the many times my grandmother had told me passionately of Hungary's once-great empire. "We used to have a navy!" she would say fiercely, an index finger pointing skyward. Another typically Hungarian incongruity—a landlocked country ruled by an admiral.

The contradictions and evasions might have had a trace of comedy, if the circumstances had not turned out so tragically. The Germans acted with single-mindedness and speed. Adolph Eichmann, effectively the chief operator of Nazi Holocaust machinery, arrived in Hungary with a small staff amidst the German occupation. Within a matter of weeks, plans for the deportation of Hungary's Jews were finalized and, with the indispensable aid of the Hungarian national police force, the deportation had begun. By late June, one senior Hungarian official reported with satisfaction to his government that some 440,000 Jews had been deported to Auschwitz. "The healthy strong circulation of a tree cleared of the blood louse has started," said the official.

I imagined Simon and István, their wives, and their children, stuffed into one of those trains along with thousands, each suffocating car "supplied with two buckets; one filled with water and the other empty, for excrements." At the border with Czechoslovakia, the train transferred from Hungarian to German control. Then it moved on to Auschwitz and down the final meters of track. I saw them shuffle, clothed, then naked, into the gas chambers, their lifeless bodies later burned in nearby pits, where along the bottom, "a channel was dug in the center to make possible the 'harvesting' of the fat exuding from the burning corpses for reuse as fuel in the cremation."

Only the Jews of Budapest remained, and it was not difficult to sense the blue intensity of Eichmann, László Endre, Hungary's little Eichmann, and their like to finish the job. In June, Jews were concentrated in Yellow Star houses, fear filling the city as action in Budapest was expected any day. Finally, roused partly by a few of the nobles who had appealed to his sense of honor and Magyar pride, Horthy ordered an end to the deportations. A cat-and-mouse game played out over the summer, with deportations scheduled, then postponed. Near summer's end, Romania withdrew from its alliance with Germany, made peace with the Soviets, and joined the attack on German and Hungarian forces. Fearful of a similar move by Hungary, the Nazis acceded to Horthy's demand, canceled deportations, and recalled Eichmann to Germany.

I felt hungry in the early afternoon, but the more I read, the more the hunger abated, until it vanished under a low-level nausea that coated my stomach. The history brought to mind family. As with Simon and István and their journey to Auschwitz, where my mind did not have family story to draw upon, it filled in with imagination, and where imagination failed, there were only questions.

I looked out at the Broadway median and watched a small group of older Caribbean men as they sat on one of the benches. One man shot his arms out and waved them around. Then he brought his hands together in a clap and, though I could not hear them through the window, the others threw back their heads in extended laughter.

I wondered about my grandmother's state of mind late that summer. I pictured the move from Bulyovszky utca, where she and Alexander had married and raised their children, to the Jewish Star building on Arany János utca. I saw her scuttle out one early morning to buy food and watched her speaking quietly with the aunts over after-dinner coffee, one of their few remaining luxuries. The converted aunts were assured in their ability to survive. What was the look on their faces as she sought their counsel? Was it condescension? Pity? I saw her furtive meetings with her best friend, a Christian, as they confirmed their shared beliefs about what had really happened in the countryside, what really awaited the Jews of Budapest, and later as they began to work through the details of how to obtain false papers for my grandmother. I saw the young Maria seated in bed in her nightgown, book in hand, a pleasant, even sensual smile on her face. And then I saw her that August of 1944, reflecting on the events of the previous fifteen months since the death of her life's love. He had provided. He had filled the family with life. He had protected. Now the roles had passed to her, and the young woman in the bedroom photo was hardened by necessity into a taker of bold risks, a cool schemer. Where she once might have trusted in authority without thinking, now she mistrusted nearly everyone and everything, putting faith only in her own judgment and actions. Circumstances were forcing her to choose between compliance and resistance. I thought of the copy of Eve's conversion certificate, obtained in September 1944, anticipated her placement for hiding in the convent, and saw my grandmother move decisively toward resistance.

But the history was sickening me, and the instinctive identification with my family wore my emotions. It was long past lunch. I got up to refill my tea and to get something sweet to force into my system. As I waited in line, I could not shake the spring and summer of 1944, the facts of history, the fragments of family story. They intermingled and began to assemble into pieces. The more they did so, and the more the pieces began to suggest a whole, the more I sensed my grandmother becoming a memory.

I thanked the barista and wound my way back to my seat. A group of older men, looking and sounding like retired Columbia professors, had gathered at the table next to mine.

"Impeachment?" said one. "For parsing the definition of 'is'? Come on."

"Now Nixon," said another in outraged agreement. "He was—"

I sat down and studied the tenements on the other side of Broadway as I ate. It was about the same time of year the Budapest Jews had been forced to move, and I found myself assessing which of the buildings across the way might have made good Yellow Star houses. Then I returned to Braham and the fall of 1944.

Horthy's proclamation of peace with the Soviets was read over Hungarian radio at one o'clock in the afternoon on October 15th. Within hours, the Germans arrested Horthy and installed a puppet government of Hungarian Nazis. The Arrow Cross, or Nyilas, as they were known, lost little time unleashing party gangs on Jews across the city. Eichmann returned, and there followed a series of official announcements and actions aimed at rounding up Jews. In the early morning hours of October 20th, Nyilas and police forces entered Jewish buildings. Men age sixteen to sixty were told to be ready to leave in one hour. I saw my father shivering in the courtyard. Two days later, there was another order that included women ages eighteen to forty. Nearly thirty-five thousand men and women complied and were taken away.

My grandmother was thirty-nine, and by this time almost certainly had false papers, had gone into hiding, and had placed my father in the orphanage. Over the next eight weeks she tended to the children, and perhaps paid brief visits to friends and the aunts, as pressure and violence escalated. The Jews who had assembled in response to the official orders were marched west toward Austria, along the road to Hegyeshalom to build up Vienna's defenses, or to the Mauthausen death camp. Tales of the starvation and murder that occurred during the marches must have swirled back to Budapest. In early December, all Jews were ordered into a ghetto established in the Jewish quarter, and within a few weeks some seventy thousand had gathered there. Many thousands remained in hiding, emboldened perhaps by the advance of Soviet troops. Shortly after Christmas, the Red Army encircled the city. In the chaos that ensued, no one was safe.

> The reign of terror that had begun with Szálasi's assumption of power on October 15 went almost completely out of control after the beginning of the Soviet siege. Gangs of armed Nyilas roamed Budapest and the other territories under their control, looting and killing defenseless victims and above all Jews.... The gangs, consisting mostly of teenagers, roamed around the city hunting for Jews 'in hiding.' They attacked Jews huddled in their shelters, cellars, and homes outside the ghetto, in the international ghetto, and in the large ghetto. Their attacks became increasingly daring and ever larger in scale.... Usually the Jews were first robbed of their last remaining valuables. Many were shot on the spot; others were taken to the banks of the Danube and shot into the river. The method of execution was to tie three people together, place them at the edge of the Danube, and shoot the middle one in the back of his head at close range so that the weight of his body would pull the other two living victims into the river.

Eve was pulled from the convent and hidden with friends, first in their apartment, and later in the basement wood closet. My father was taken from the orphanage and placed in another building. After the Soviets closed all exit from the city, they attacked. The block-by-block battle involved some of the fiercest urban fighting of the war. Had she herself been stopped by the youth gangs? How much had she increased their risk of exposure when she brought my father close after he could stand the separation no more? On January 8th, the head of the Jewish Council and one hundred fifty-four others were taken by the Nyilas from 4 Üllűi út. She had brought my father to her cellar on Üllűi út. I pictured him venturing to the courtyard, where he sipped stew handed him by a friendly German, watching as the cook butchered a horse and prepared a fresh batch.

Then it was over. They returned to the apartment on Arany János utca as the last of the Germans fought to the death in the Buda hills above. The Soviets occupied the city. In the fall, the children went back to school. My grandmother opened a fabric store on the Vaci utca in the heart of downtown. And my father became an altar boy at St. Stephen's cathedral, the largest in Budapest. There he experienced the rapturous relationship with God he had told me about, a spiritual encounter he would never have again. At an abstract level, I understood. Probably to no small degree, the Holy Father replaced his departed father. Still, I felt guilt and confusion as Braham's text echoed in my mind. "The method of execution was to tie three people together, place them at the edges of the Danube, and shoot the middle one in the back of the head at close range, so that the weight of his body would pull the other two living victims into the river."

I looked with suspicion on the crowd around me, my anxiety sharpened by a sudden wave of claustrophobia. I got up, went outside, and breathed in the early summer air. Had they heard the screams as the Nyilas pulled innocent victims from nearby building cellars? Had they heard the final pleas, the riverbank gunshots? They had survived — my grandmother, Eve, and my father. Why? Many people had been cunning and courageous. Chance had favored fewer. But there was another factor, assimilation.

I pictured my grandfather in his fabric store, smoking a cigarette my grandmother had rolled for him that morning, cracking jokes with his cousin. It was late winter in early 1943. He had walked his son to school that morning, dropping him there after a brief vomiting episode. My father sat in class daydreaming of the games he would play with friends that afternoon. They must have felt secure beneath their cloak of assimilation, I concluded. But then I wondered how completely they had embraced it. Eve had been baptized in 1939. Was this a long-delayed wish on the part of my grandparents, or a calculated step to hedge risks in the wake of anti-Jewish laws? I thought of my father's arrival at the Jesuit school in the fall after his father died, how when registering with the police, he had told them his religion was Israelite. If he had been converted, he would have entered "Catholic." And yet, if Eve had been converted, why had not he been, too? I experienced their assimilation as my own for a moment, and then saw my father at the Jesuit boarding school, breaking the ice on his wash basin, dressing to meet his uncle for the train back to Budapest, wondering why he was being removed from school. I did not know who first pinned the Yellow Star upon his jacket, but I imagined that it was his uncle on that train ride. Jostled by passengers shoehorned around him, fear and tumult coursing through the crowded train, I saw my father staring at the bright yellow object on his chest, not understanding.

The nuns took in Eve, the convert. My father inhabited his Christian identity effortlessly. The children could be excused. They might not have understood what was happening. But my grandmother had, and I questioned how, after the war, after all that had happened, she could let my father go to that church, don those robes.

I heard my grandmother's words again, "Sixty friends and family." They lived, even as the sixty had gone to Auschwitz, were killed in labor service in the army, left dead by the highway to Hegyeshalom, or were shot into the icy, night-black Danube. Who were the cousins and companions, people who had shared meals, outings, holidays? Beyond Simon and István, there were dozens about whom I knew nothing. I imagined them all together, walking down a Budapest street in heavy coats and shawls, belongings on their backs or in bulky suitcases hastily packed, their eyes worried or numb. What were their names? Where had they lived? What were they like? Did she recall the last time she had seen them? My longing to ask her was profound. But she could no longer answer.

[40]

She made only meager progress in physical therapy. Then her hospitalization benefits ran out and she had to be moved. The obvious alternative was a rehabilitation center in Westchester that was run by the mother-in-law of one of Eve's daughters. It promised attentive care and progress. But she had a minor stroke during her transfer to the center and another not long after she arrived, pushing her recovery still further from our grasp. "She's worse," was all my father would say.

I buried myself in work and tried to avoid thinking about her. This attempt at numbing succeeded incompletely, and one mild and cloudless November Saturday I drove up with Norah to see her. After several wrong turns, we found the center, a plain, two-story building with a bland brick exterior and simple square windows, tucked into a small parcel of land at the junction of two busy highways. Across the street was the local hospital, a 1950s style monolith, and, stepping from the car, I stared at it until the loud grinding of a downshifting eighteen-wheeler broke the soothing din of interstate traffic. In the lobby, a colorful menagerie of tropical fish darted about a large tank. Norah sat on a stiff couch as a squat, red-cheeked nurse looked up Granny's name and signed us in.

As I came off the elevator, I nearly bumped into two attendants in maroon hospital-style outfits. I stopped a nurse and she gestured toward a long hallway, the shiny linoleum floor reflecting the white fluorescent lights. We passed the TV room, where a stadium crowd and an excited sports announcer blared as someone scored a touchdown. Many of the twenty or so old people sitting around the television did not seem to notice. Some chatted in pairs, a few napped, others directed blank stares at the game. Two old women and a man sat in wheelchairs in the hall. The man wore a tired expression, and sparse stubble dotted his cheeks and chin. He spoke a few words to one of the women. I strained to hear what he was saying as we passed and almost tripped over Granny.

She was slumped in a wheelchair, eyes closed. A rolling stand held a feeding bag filled with beige-colored liquid. The tube from the bag vanished into her light blue gown. I tapped her lightly on the shoulder and she began to roll her head back and forth. She lifted her eyelids and closed them, then she blinked. Her eyes were watery and fixed at something invisible to her left.

"You need to stand over here," said a nurse as she passed, prodding me to Granny's right. "She can see you better there."

I stepped into her skewed field of vision, and she moved her lips and gurgled. She lowered her eyes. I kneeled down and touched her hand, "Yes, it's me," I said, "and Norah's here, too." She turned her head and nodded at Norah. "I brought you some pictures," I said.

We wheeled her into her room and I sat on the bed across from her. I flipped through the stack of photos of our summer vacation and some snapshots of my nephew that my sister had sent, feeling a disorienting jumble of affection and repulsion, happiness and despair. I chatted about the different scenes, trying to maintain a positive tone as she shifted her gaze to the bare wall behind me. Her eyes grew heavy, and soon she was dozing. I began to sweat and kept speaking, hoping she would rouse herself.

"Oh, hey, this one's great. Benjamin, your grandson, in a stroller with Nancy in the park in the Netherlands."

She snored.

"Granny," I said, putting the picture back on the pile. Then, again, "Granny." Her eyes popped open and she blinked. "Would you like to go outside?"

She bowed her head.

After checking with the attendant, we rolled her down to the back patio. I positioned her so that she was a little out of the shade, the warm fall sun on her back. "Do you feel the sun? It's just right today," I said. She nodded. Norah took out the pictures and showed them to her again. I stared at the traffic just on the other side of a row of evergreens, my mind empty. Then Granny broke my trance. "Hot," she said. "Hot."

I got up and wheeled her into the shade near some sliding doors that led into an all-purpose room. One of the doors opened, and a heavyset, middle-aged woman in a light yellow sweater and black slacks stepped out onto the patio, shading her eyes and squinting. She was humming scales and smiled at us before strolling back inside, where she spoke with two men, one at a piano and the other tuning a guitar. Residents began filling the rows of seats in front of the musicians.

I pulled up a chair next to Granny and Norah and sat down. The three of us watched bits of cars and trucks flicker through the vegetation. Granny stirred, and as I looked over, our eyes met. She said something I could not understand. "Girls?" I said, straining to decipher the sounds.

She paused, then tried again. "Different worlds," she slurred.

I nodded. "Yes, different worlds."

We found space near the back of the all-purpose room. The woman from the patio picked up a microphone and broke into a broad smile. "Hello everyone!" A few residents mumbled greetings and she shook her head and cupped her hand behind her ear. "Hell-o every-one!" she shouted.

"Hello!" came the response, louder and peppered with good-natured chuckles.

"I'm Deb Wilson and we're After Five," she said, as the musicians waved to the crowd. "We're going to do some oldies and some goodies for you, and we hope you will join in!" Then she turned to the band and launched into a jazzy version of "Somewhere Over the Rainbow." Despite some lags in rhythm and a few off-key notes, when the song was over, the crowd offered warm applause. The audience was overwhelmingly female, their husbands having passed years before. Near us a lively group of white-haired women in flower-print blouses had pulled their chairs into a semicircle. Here and there, a number of people sat alone. Behind us, a grizzled man in a wheelchair stared at the floor. "I want to wake up in a city that doesn't sleep, no, no!" the singer chanted. Granny tapped her good right hand against her left forearm. I reached over and straightened the small blanket on her lap.

"Wonderful!" exclaimed a large woman in the front row in a loud dress and a wide, straw hat. "You should be on Broadway! How about 'Oklahoma' or 'Let's Call the Whole Thing Off'?"

"Oh well, we'll see," said the singer, pleased. The front-row lady continued to holler encouragement and requests as the band made its way through old show tunes and kitschy pop hits. The musicians smiled more and more enthusiastically with each generous round of applause, and as they played, their energy seemed to lift the crowd. I noticed that the cheeks of a few of the white-haired women in front of us had grown pink with excitement as they gazed at the musicians, dreams in their eyes.

Most of the audience hummed or sang along with the familiar songs, and Granny remained awake and alert, tapping her forearm from time to time. "Celebrate good times, come on!" the singer implored, and several residents got to their feet and clapped along with the beat. I turned to Granny, hoping to exchange a smirk, but her glassy eyes were facing the music. I stared out the sliding doors behind the musicians and thought about an opera Granny and I had once seen at the Met, then applause brought me back to the rehab center and the woman in the wide hat calling for an encore.

The show ended after a long ovation, and a din of happy voices and sliding chairs settled over the room. Some residents began to make their way to the door, and the first faint scents of an institutional lunch filtered into the room. My mind wandered to the stroll we had taken around the neighborhood near the 92nd Street Y that lovely spring day. I felt her hand on my elbow, heard her laughter as she told me the story of her cousins and the barber. I saw her emerge from the building cellar with my father after the air raid, watched them wander the destruction. I imagined her again on that bench atop Riverside Park, meditating on the Hudson and her predicament with Emery. How much more she deserved, this wreck now sitting beside me. I stood up. Norah glanced at me as she sat stroking Granny's arm. I walked quickly through the milling crowd, shifted in the elevator, impatient, and grabbed our coats from Granny's room. I returned, sat down next to Granny, and was just about to say a terse goodbye when she lifted her head, tilted it toward me, and said, in a hoarse near-whisper, "Help me."

[41]

Late one night, not long after the nursing home visit, I labored at the dining table on a report, my notes and references scattered about, a small desk lamp providing a cone of light. I put my pen down and checked the bookshelf clock. It was nearly one in the morning. My eyes caught sight of the binder of Braham's material, and I chuckled darkly. How backward it had all been, my desire to learn coming after it was possible to get answers to so many more questions. Why can't wisdom come before experience? I asked half-seriously. The image of Granny slumped in a wheelchair entered my mind. Then her nursing home plea. I closed my eyes and shook my head but could not expel the vision, the sound. I rose and began flipping through a drawer of cassette tapes in the TV console. I found what I was looking for near the back, snapped it into the cassette player, and slipped on a set of headphones. The clink of glasses and background clatter transported me to Moca and our discussion of her escape from Hungary.

"We got off the train in the city of Satoraljaujhely," she said. "The girlfriend of one of the smugglers came with us from Budapest. I gave her a pair of diamond earrings to pay her for the trip." The words flowed through me, and I listened harder. "We walked to the highway until a car came. That was by prior arrangement." Tenor-saxophone-like tones, an irregular, syncopated cadence, vast energy. "The car stopped. 'Would you like to take a ride?' That was the driver. 'We are very tired,' I answered." She laughed radiant staccato blasts. "He took us somewhere near the border of Czechoslovakia where there was a group of people already hiding in the woods. It was a dark night. I paid the driver three thousand forint. A man looking like a bum came out of the woods, then we started walking. We walked all night."

The words melted and the pure sound of her voice filled me. I had the vague awareness that she lost her money and her coat, and yet even in moments such as these, the voice had a range of color, an electricity, that contented me. Difficult experience had given her a passionate voice, not a deflated one. So alive, I thought to myself.

In the background the story passed — a drive across Czechoslovakia, a night in a roadside ditch as Russians rumbled by, Vienna, Emery — but it barely registered. I embraced the warm sensation of the voice, curled up and rested beside it. I embraced her memory and a thought flitted through my mind — to hold her I had to let go. "Oh Granny," I said aloud. The headphones amplified the sound of my voice, and I noticed a strange new harmony in its tone, a mix of sadness, bittersweet joy, and wonder. I grew drowsy, crossed my arms on the table, and laid my head down.

[42]

Months after she moved to the rehabilitation center, months of silent suffering, months in which lucidity vanished, months alone, too many months, she died. The phone rang and I put breakfast down and hurried to answer it. I drew my breath at late-night and early-morning calls, anticipating my mother's voice and my father's collapse.

"Pete," my father said.

"Dad. Good morning!" My tone was cheery, yet I knew as soon as he spoke.

"It's my mother. She died during the night."

"Oh, no," I said, but I was relieved to hear his voice, relieved the end had come. It seemed pointless to ask for the details, and he began giving me information about the funeral.

"Pauli is in Washington, I am in Washington. She should be down there," said my father, growing agitated as he stood in the middle of the funeral home.

"Dani, she spent her life in New York and who was there all the time for her?" said Eve, jabbing a finger in her chest, "Me."

"You? You terrified her with your nonsense when she stayed with you."

Many in the small crowd looked over at the bickering pair.

"Ridiculous," said Eve, her voice quieting as she glanced around. "She loved to visit us."

I was reluctant to say anything, astonished that they had not yet decided what to do with her ashes, afraid of how they might respond to the idea that had just come to me. But I spoke up.

"What if you divided her?" I offered.

The two of them turned and stared at me.

And that is what they did. One portion of the ashes was buried near Eve, just outside New York. A second measure went into a niche in a cemetery not far from my father. And one evening the following week, cousin Eva boarded a Malev jet and returned to Budapest with the last bit of dust in her purse. Not long after, Eva took the trolley out to the Kozma Street Cemetery and planted marigolds and petunias on Alexander's grave, as she did each spring at Granny's request. When she was done, she pulled the small tin from her bag and sprinkled the ashes over the soil.

Granny would have been horrified by the division, and enthralled by it, too. I imagine the two of us hunched over coffee cups in a noisy restaurant as I tell her the story and watch her shout, "Terrible! Terrible!" in between long, laughter-soaked breaths.

AUTHOR'S NOTE

Many people provided help along the way as this book evolved, and I want to express my deep appreciation to them. Pierre Epstein and Jeff Garigliano offered tolerant and thoughtful feedback at the start. Claudia Kalb and Nancy Szabo reviewed early drafts, and David Groff provided critical developmental guidance and encouragement. Nancy Bailey lent a sure copyediting hand. Steven Drachman at Chickadee Prince Books gave his wisdom and attention to detail to the publishing process. We are all in debt to Randolph Braham for his work to document the Hungarian Holocaust, and I thank him, additionally, for permission to quote from his book, *The Politics of Genocide: The Holocaust in Hungary*. My Aunt, Eve Malecki, served up delicious marzipan cake along with her memories and commentary. My father, Daniel Szabo, was open and generous in interviews and when responding to many follow-up questions. My wife Norah was extraordinarily patient and supportive.

Most of all, I am grateful to Maria, for her friendship, her love, and her example.

Peter Szabo
September 2016